Praise for
Be Well, Learn Well

'*Be Well, Learn Well* is an excellent toolkit for navigating university, packed with useful and practical ideas to help students look after their mental wellbeing and learn effectively. A must-read for any student!'

— **Elena Riva**, *University of Warwick, UK*

'This book is informative, engaging and research-informed, and the friendly tone makes it very accessible to students. It includes a wide range of practical study and wellbeing strategies, making it very useful for all students and also relevant to the staff who support them.'

— **Anthony Payne**, *Director of Student Services, University of Bath, UK*

'As they go through education, many young people imbibe the idea that their mental health is completely unrelated to, or even at odds with, their academic learning. What Gareth Hughes has done with this book is not only to thoroughly debunk this myth using solid evidence, but also show practical ways students can avoid burnout, and improve both their learning and health outcomes. I really wish I'd had a copy of this before I went to uni.'

— **Natasha Devon MBE**, author of *Yes You Can: ...ut Losing Your Mind*

www.thestudyspace.com – the leading study skills website

Study Skills

Academic Success
Academic Writing Skills for International
  Students
The Business Student's Phrase Book
Cite Them Right (11th edn)
Critical Thinking and Persuasive Writing for
  Postgraduates
Critical Thinking Skills (3rd edn)
Dissertations and Project Reports
Doing Projects and Reports in Engineering
The Employability Journal
Essentials of Essay Writing
The Exam Skills Handbook (2nd edn)
Get Sorted
The Graduate Career Guidebook (2nd edn)
Great Ways to Learn Anatomy and Physiology
  (2nd edn)
How to Begin Studying English Literature
  (4th edn)
How to Use Your Reading in Your Essays (3rd edn)
How to Write Better Essays (4th edn)
How to Write Your Undergraduate Dissertation
  (3rd edn)
Improve Your Grammar (2nd edn)
The Mature Student's Guide to Writing (3rd edn)
The Mature Student's Handbook
Mindfulness for Students
The Macmillan Student Planner
The Personal Tutor's Handbook
Presentation Skills for Students (3rd edn)
The Principles of Writing in Psychology
Professional Writing (4th edn)
Reading at University
Simplify Your Study
Skills for Success (3rd edn)
Stand Out from the Crowd
The Student Phrase Book (2nd edn)
The Student's Guide to Writing (3rd edn)
Study Skills Connected
The Study Skills Handbook (5th edn)
Study Skills for International Postgraduates
Studying in English
Studying History (4th edn)
Studying Law (4th edn)
Studying Physics
The Study Success Journal
Success in Academic Writing (2nd edn)
Smart Thinking
Teaching Study Skills and Supporting Learning
The Undergraduate Research Handbook (2nd edn)
The Work-Based Learning Student Handbook
  (2nd edn)
Writing for Biomedical Sciences Students

Writing for Engineers (4th edn)
Writing History Essays (2nd edn)
Writing for Law
Writing for Nursing and Midwifery Students
  (3rd edn)
Write it Right (2nd edn)
Writing for Science Students
Writing Skills for Education Students
You2Uni: Decide, Prepare, Apply

Pocket Study Skills

14 Days to Exam Success (2nd edn)
Analyzing a Case Study
Brilliant Writing Tips for Students
Completing Your PhD
Doing Research (2nd edn)
Getting Critical (2nd edn)
How to Analyze Data
Managing Stress
Planning Your Dissertation (2nd edn)
Planning Your Essay (3rd edn)
Planning Your PhD
Posters and Presentations
Reading and Making Notes (2nd edn)
Referencing and Understanding Plagiarism
  (2nd edn)
Reflective Writing
Report Writing (2nd edn)
Science Study Skills
Studying with Dyslexia (2nd edn)
Success in Groupwork
Successful Applications
Time Management
Using Feedback to Boost Your Grades
Where's Your Argument?
Where's Your Evidence?
Writing for University (2nd edn)

Research Skills

Authoring a PhD
The Foundations of Research (3rd edn)
Getting to Grips with Doctoral Research
Getting Published
The Good Supervisor (2nd edn)
The Lean PhD
PhD by Published Work
The PhD Viva
The PhD Writing Handbook
Planning Your Postgraduate Research
The Postgraduate's Guide to Research Ethics
The Postgraduate Research Handbook (2nd edn)
The Professional Doctorate
Structuring Your Research Thesis

For a complete listing of all our titles in this area please visit
www.macmillanihe.com/study-skills

Be Well, Learn Well

Improve Your Wellbeing and Academic Performance

Gareth Hughes

macmillan
international
HIGHER EDUCATION

RED GLOBE
PRESS

First published 2020 by
RED GLOBE PRESS

Red Globe Press in the UK is an imprint of Macmillan Education Limited, registered in England, company number 01755588, of 4 Crinan Street, London, N1 9XW.

Red Globe Press® is a registered trademark in the United States, the United Kingdom, Europe and other countries.

ISBN 978-1-352-01068-8 paperback

This book is printed on paper suitable for recycling and made from fully managed and sustained forest sources. Logging, pulping and manufacturing processes are expected to conform to the environmental regulations of the country of origin.

A catalogue record for this book is available from the British Library.

A catalog record for this book is available from the Library of Congress.

Contents

Foreword

It is a true privilege to be asked to introduce *Be Well, Learn Well*. Having experienced my own ups and downs whilst trying to discover how to 'be well' and 'learn well', I wish I could have read this book when preparing to go to university.

My understanding of how my mind, wellbeing and learning relate clicked into place in March 2016, the first time I listened to a talk by the author of *Be Well, Learn Well*, Gareth Hughes.

I still remember listening to Gareth's story about how students on a gaming course had learnt how to build their wellbeing using the creative and challenging scenario of managing the launch of a video game. Gareth's practical, honest and encouraging reflections about how all students can learn at their best, by tapping into what they care about, really resonated with me and the experience I'd had during my degree when I shifted from simply trying to pass exams to caring deeply about my subject.

It's fantastic to see these ideas and more expanded upon in this book. I am a big believer that a book can change your life. This is true when it's a book based on solid evidence, practical experience and students' lives – like this one.

Gareth is a passionate advocate for student wellbeing and someone that I'm very proud to call a good friend and collaborator. The projects that I have collaborated on with Gareth and the wonderful team at Student Minds (the UK's student mental health charity) have been the most fulfilling. Of particular note is the development of the University Mental Health Charter, a quality improvement and award scheme which, thanks to a small team of committed people and thousands of students and staff from the higher education community, will create environments where all of us can thrive. Creating structural and cultural change is necessary, but the truth is that in order to create a better world and build the lives and careers we want for ourselves and others, we need to recognise that the change starts with us.

Positive change, which is all the more needed against the challenging backdrop of the Covid-19 outbreak in 2020, starts when all of us learn about our health and wellbeing.

I've learnt that my ability to lead an organisation is very much reliant on whether I can achieve the good balance of fun, rest and work that this book discusses, challenge my own unhelpful critical thoughts, reflect on my mistakes and develop a positive self-belief. I'm still working on these, but thanks to the tools and techniques in this book, I'm getting there!

All of us can learn something from this book. Whether you're preparing for your exams at school, your first university group project or your first week in the graduate workplace or, like me, you're a professional looking for positive and effective ways to empower students, all of us can keep learning how to be well and learn well. The world needs us to.

Rosie Tressler, OBE
CEO, Student MindsHow to use this book

How to use this book

I know that, as a student, you already have lots to read. So this book has been designed so that you can use it in the way that is most helpful for you.

If you want to read it from cover to cover, that's great. You'll get a really in-depth understanding of the concepts around wellbeing and learning and lots of ideas on things you can do to ensure you feel well and learn well. For those of you who are keen to know more, I've also provided references and some suggested further reading.

But if you want to use the contents page as a menu, so you can dip in and out of the bits that are most helpful to you, that's great too. If in one chapter there is something that we talk about in another, I've made sure this is clearly signposted so you can follow up on it.

Throughout this book, I've included a lot of suggestions for ways in which you can improve your wellbeing and learning. As you are reading, you may find it useful to note down anything that you find interesting, would like to try for yourself or would like to know more about. That way, as you read on, you won't forget what it was that sparked your interest. To help you with this, I've included a worksheet at the back of the book, where you can note down anything you want to come back to, and a space for any notes you want to make for yourself.

Introduction

Making the most of university

Imagine the following scenario –

You wake up on a chilly, dark morning in winter. You have a cold; your head hurts and your nose is blocked. You get up and drag yourself to the shower, but because you aren't feeling well, getting ready takes longer and you don't have time for breakfast. You get into university and into your first class of the day, only to discover that your two best friends are also ill and have decided to stay at home. Feeling a little lonely, hungry, ill and cold, you settle down at a desk by yourself. You don't like the class that is about to begin, and you find the subject boring.

How much learning do you think you'll do in this class? How easy will it be to concentrate, take in new information, make connections to things you've already learned and increase your understanding of this subject?

Now imagine this scenario –

You wake up on a sunny day, late in spring. You slept well the night before and feel refreshed and full of energy. You eat your favourite breakfast and then head into university for your favourite class, on a subject that you're passionate about. As you wait for class to start, you chat to your two best friends and make plans for fun things you'll do this weekend.

How much learning will you do in this class? How easy will it be to concentrate, take in new information, make connections to things you've already learned and increase your understanding of this subject?

When put like this, it's easy to say that you will probably learn more in the second scenario. When we're feeling full of energy and enthusiasm, it is much easier to learn and perform well than when we feel ill, tired, upset, hungry or lonely. When we set these two scenarios together like this, it is easy to see how our wellbeing can impact on our learning and academic performance.

But now let's ask another question – when you usually think about your learning and academic achievement, how often do you think about the role your wellbeing played in how much you learned or in the grades you got?

For many of the students that I've worked with over the years, when they think about what might determine their academic learning and performance, their wellbeing comes way behind other thoughts (if at all). Most students tend to focus on their own academic ability, the quality of the teaching they received, how much work they did, the practical things that got in the way or helped them, and luck.

For those students who do think about the role their wellbeing has played, it's often because something very obvious happened – they fell ill just before an exam or they experienced severe exam anxiety, for instance.

Other students may be aware that improving their wellbeing might help their learning, but they don't yet know how to make positive changes that will stick.

The relationship between our wellbeing and our learning can be one of those things we sort of know about but don't think about or prioritise. As a result, we can slip into behaviours and habits that mean we learn less and, as a result, get less enjoyment out of being a student.

Luckily, there are many ways to improve your wellbeing and your learning.

Taking control

Although we can't control everything that happens to us, we often have more influence over our wellbeing than we realise. Even in difficult circumstances, there are usually things we can do to support our wellbeing. How we feel isn't determined entirely by what happens in the world around us.

Of course, this is very easy to say, and taking control of our wellbeing is often more difficult to do. Sometimes, life throws up problems and barriers to healthy activities or we may not know how to take control of our particular circumstances. Even with the best of intentions, we sometimes start out planning to do something that is good for us and then find we have slipped back into old unhealthy habits.

How many of us have tried to adopt a healthier diet or spend less time on our phone and then realised that we are eating our way through a bar of chocolate or spending hours on Instagram?

What is true for our wellbeing is also true for our learning and academic performance. Even when we recognise that we could improve our skills, understanding and ability, finding the motivation to practise, work more or seek out support can be difficult. For some students, it can also be easy to assume that our academic ability is fixed and therefore that there is no point in trying to improve.

In this book, we will explore different ways to improve both your wellbeing and your learning. It is absolutely possible to do both – sometimes with the same intervention. Because our wellbeing and learning are linked, when you improve one, you can frequently improve the other as well.

Holistic model of learning and wellbeing

Performance of any kind is heavily influenced by a whole range of factors. Think about athletes in almost any professional sport. They don't just practise the skills they need; they also make sure they are eating the right diet, getting enough sleep and resting. They need to have good relationships around them, whether that means bonding with teammates or making sure there is unity with their coaching team. Finally, top athletes devote time to ensuring that they have a positive mind-set and good self-belief.

These things matter for our ability to produce good performance. Just look at the number of soccer teams at the World Cup that are full of brilliant players but go on to underperform because the squad is divided, unhappy or bored.

The same is true of academic performance.

Take a look at the figure below [1].

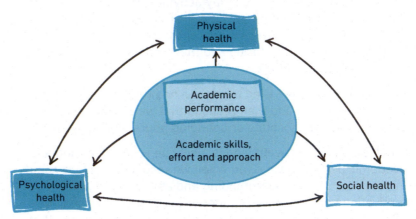

This shows how physical health, psychological health and social health – when added to academic ability, effort and approach to learning – produce your overall academic performance.

But the model also shows two other important things.

First of all, the arrows run in both directions – not only does your wellbeing influence learning and performance but learning and performance also have an impact on your wellbeing. (In **Chapter 4**, we'll look at how this works – but for now, just think about how a poor exam result can affect your psychological wellbeing.)

Second, each of these domains of wellbeing also affects each other. For example, your physical health impacts on your mood and your social health. Just think of times when you've felt ill; when this happens, it isn't unusual for someone to feel emotionally down or irritable and to want to withdraw from other people until they feel well again. Sometimes, we can think about different aspects of ourselves as though they are unconnected. For instance, we may think that how we are managing our physical wellbeing and how we are performing academically are two completely separate things. But they are not – all of these things are constantly influencing each other.

So, if you want to improve your learning, it is worth looking at ways of improving your skills or increasing the amount of effort you're putting in – we'll look at this in **Chapter 4**.

But depending on your circumstances, you might also gain from getting better sleep or spending more time with friends.

Throughout the rest of this book, we'll look at how we can make improvements in each of these areas and we'll examine some of the evidence that shows us how improving our wellbeing can improve our learning and vice versa.

Before that, there are some key principles that are worth bearing in mind.

1. Nothing works for everyone – but everyone can find something that works for them

One of the great things about people is that we are all different from each other. Our diversity makes the world a better and more interesting place – but it also means that we respond differently to the same thing. You can see this really clearly when we look at interventions to help people who are experiencing problems with their mental health. If you look at the evidence from clinical trials and from practice, you will see that no treatment can resolve things for 100% of the population. Some will get better with one type of therapy, some from another and some will get no benefit from any type of therapy but may benefit from support to change their lifestyle.

This means that if you've already tried something and it hasn't worked, don't get downhearted. It just means you haven't found the right thing for you – yet. If you keep experimenting and use support, you will find an approach that works for you.

2. Small steps win the race

When you want to improve things in your life, it can be tempting to throw everything overboard and to try to change everything at once. Unfortunately, what tends to happen when we do this is that we get overwhelmed, slip back into old habits and then give up. Human beings are generally creatures of habit and we will gravitate back to what we know, in terms of routine, even when it is bad for us.

That's why it is important to begin by taking a few small, positive and achievable steps that help you to meet your needs in a more healthy way. By focussing on one or two small steps, you are more likely to make sustainable improvements that stick. Once you have made these into new habits, you can add some more steps, building positive momentum as you go.

3. Use the support around you

Universities put a lot of support in place to help their students. What this support looks like will be different depending on your university and the country where you are based. But one thing remains true no matter where you study: there are staff in your institution that only exist to help you be successful. People like me have no other purpose in being there – we want to work with you and help you to reach your potential and thrive as a student. That can be true of your lecturers, the library staff, the teams in student services or student affairs, the careers departments, the accommodation staff and on and on and on.

But being at university means you are in charge of your learning and your journey. You are in control. We put a lot of support around you but it's for you to use it when it can help most. That means staff won't necessarily approach you to offer support unless you ask for it first.

Don't worry if this feels overwhelming or if you are someone who finds it difficult to ask for help. Identifying the support you need and asking for it are skills, and like all skills they can be improved with practice.

Asking for support is a strength, not a sign of weakness. We say that 'successful students use support' – they identify areas for improvement, access the support that can help them and as a result learn more, feel better and perform better. You can learn how to do this in time.

Reference

1 Hughes, G. & Wilson, C. (2017). From Transcendence to General Maintenance: Exploring the Creativity and Wellbeing Dynamic in Higher Education. In: F. Reisman (Ed.), *Creativity, Innovation and Wellbeing*. London: KIE Conference Publications, pp. 23–65.

2

What is 'wellbeing' and why is it important to you?

If you look for images related to the word 'wellbeing' on an internet search engine, a number of common themes pop up, none of them necessarily all that helpful.

The first type of image is a picture of a young woman, usually in a vest, doing yoga outdoors, with her eyes closed. Sometimes, the woman is in a field or near a tree, but most often she is on a beach. The sun is shining, and she seems at peace.

The second type of image shows several young people doing something active – jumping into the air seems particularly popular. Some of these people are also wearing vests. At this point, the scientists among you may be wondering whether the vests are creating wellbeing somehow and that perhaps this is a hypothesis that needs to be tested.

This question is answered by the third type of image, in which there are no people but possibly some pebbles stacked on top of each other or some flowers. Neither the pebbles nor the flowers are wearing vests.

So, why are we spending time looking at these images of 'wellbeing'? Well, partly, I think, because they capture one of the problems that we all encounter when we try to think about our wellbeing and how it can be improved. Terms like 'wellbeing' and 'health' can be vague and nebulous, and as a result it can be difficult for us to figure out what we can do to make things better.

These online images don't really offer us anything practical that we might do or help us to understand what wellbeing actually is. That isn't the fault of the photographers; they're struggling with the same problem – how do you understand and demonstrate good wellbeing? But we do need to be careful not to be swayed by these images –there is a danger that we think good wellbeing is something that is possible only when conditions are perfect.

We might, for instance, find ourselves thinking:

> 'How can I possibly have good wellbeing if I can't do yoga on a beach for two hours every day?'

Instead, we need solid practical ways to think about our wellbeing which help us to identify tangible real-life steps we can take to make ourselves feel and learn better, no matter where we are or what is happening in our lives. We may not be able to have a moment of perfect wellbeing, as the rays of a setting sun caress our faces, but we can do something to make our situation better, even if only by a little bit.

We started to break down the idea of wellbeing in **Chapter 1**, where we looked at the physical, psychological, social and academic dimensions of student wellbeing. We're going to break that down even further now, using the evidence and latest ideas from the literature.

It's worth bearing in mind that how we think about things often affects what we think is possible and how we behave. If we think something is achievable, can see a route forward and believe it will benefit us, we are more willing to expend effort in trying to achieve it. If, on the other hand, we believe it is impossible or have no idea where to start, then we might not even try. Having a concrete idea of what wellbeing is and how we can practically improve it makes us more likely to take positive action.

Defining wellbeing

People have been trying to define wellbeing since as far back as classical antiquity. Thinkers such as Plato [1] and Aristotle [2] discussed the concept of 'eudaimonia', which often is translated as happiness, wellbeing or flourishing.

Aristotle argued that eudaimonia came from doing and living well and that all of this came from living life in balance.

More recently, scholars have taken a range of approaches to defining wellbeing across a number of disciplines, including psychology, philosophy, psychotherapy and economics. However, all of these approaches touch on a key issue that goes all the way back to something raised by the ancient Greeks. When we try to understand how to live a life that makes us well and in which we learn well, we first have to understand who we are as human beings.

A big question

Think about this for a moment – what is the difference between a rock and a rose?

If you think about it for a while, you'll be able to come up with a number of differences – for instance, the rock is hard whereas the rose is not. The rose is more likely to be colourful, etc.

But one of the key differences is simply this: the rose is alive; the rock is not. In fact, there is a whole branch of scientific enquiry devoted to working out how to know whether something is alive or not. One of the key ways to know if something is living is to look at what it needs to survive. For a rose to stay alive, it needs sunlight, water and nutritious soil. The rock, on the other hand, can stay largely unchanged for centuries.

Living things require various forms of nutrition to survive and thrive. We call the things we require 'needs'. You may have come across this idea before if you've ever heard of Abraham Maslow's hierarchy of needs.

Most needs theorists now agree that rather than thinking about our needs as having a hierarchy, we should focus on meeting them in balance (as Aristotle originally argued).

Maslow didn't invent the pyramid of needs

Most people who have come across Maslow's hierarchy of needs were introduced to it with the picture of a pyramid, showing each of the needs he proposed moving in order, from physiological at the bottom to self-actualisation at the top.

Although Maslow did suggest that our needs may have a hierarchy, he didn't come up with this pyramid and it doesn't feature in any of his works. Some authors claim that the pyramid itself is completely misleading and misrepresents both Maslow's theory and what we now know from research. This shows why it is always important to check your references, carefully, for yourself [3].

So what are our needs?

Various models of human needs are found in the literature, and if you want to explore this further, you can find details in the References [4–7].

Many of these frameworks are very similar, although there are differences in emphasis, language and the exact number of 'needs' that humans are perceived to have.

However, it is broadly agreed that, as humans, we have evolved a series of common needs that help us to survive and thrive. We all share the same set of needs, but how we meet them is different depending on culture, available resources and our own individual personalities, skills and preferences.

If we meet our needs in balance, we thrive; if we cannot meet our needs in balance, we experience problems such as distress or illness.

Having a framework of needs, to help us think about our wellbeing, can be very useful – especially for those times in your life when you aren't feeling good but can't quite work out why. Sometimes in therapy, I'll see a student who is experiencing anxiety or low mood with no idea what could possibly be causing them to feel this way – nothing bad has happened in their life, and they can't identify anything negative that could have caused their current emotional experiences. But when we look at how well they are meeting their needs currently, it becomes clear that the problem isn't that something has happened; it's that something is missing. Once we are able to address the needs that aren't being met, their mood returns to normal.

Thinking about your needs can also help you to work out what kind of life you want to lead. Understanding how you like to meet your needs can help you to build a life that allows you to flourish.

Human Givens theory

The model of needs that I use most often is the one derived from Human Givens theory [8]. (I'm a Human Givens psychotherapist.)

This states that we have physical and psychological needs (which are emotional and social). We will look at physical needs and wellbeing in more detail in **Chapter 3.** For now, let us consider our psychological needs.

Psychological needs

1   Security and safety

We need to feel safe and free from undue harm most of the time. For example, if you are being bullied, this can have negative impacts on your wellbeing. However, if you feel safe and supported, you are more able to be creative, take risks and grow in a healthy way.

2   Autonomy and control

We need to feel that we are in control of most of our decisions and actions and that we are able to let go of control, when that is in our best interests. Often, new students report feeling a loss of control. Finding ways to take control of what you are doing (even in small ways), such as deciding mindfully when you will see other people or eat, can help.

3   Competence and achievement

We need to feel that we are good at something and that we have something to offer the world. Hopefully, as a student, you will recognise that you are good at academic work – but you can also benefit from being good at sport or being a good friend or parent.

12   Chapter 2   What is 'wellbeing' and why is it important to you?

4   Meaning and purpose

Meaning and purpose come from being stretched and challenged by something bigger than ourselves. Learning can be a wonderful way to derive meaning – we will discuss this more in Chapter 5.

5   Friendship, love, fun and physical intimacy

Fun is important to our wellbeing overall – it helps us to relax, bond with others and feel better about life. Remember, though, that this is about balance – too much fun can interfere with our ability to meet our other needs (such as competence and achievement), but if we cut out fun to just work hard all the time, our wellbeing and then our performance will suffer.

6   Attention

Humans are not solitary creatures. We need to feel connected to other people in order to thrive. (Connection online can help build relationships with others but it isn't a substitute for face-to-face attention. We don't get the same biological payoffs from online contact.)

7   Emotional intimacy

We need to feel that there is someone else in the world who knows us and accepts us for who we are.

8   Connection to a wider community

Being connected to other people improves our immunity and seems to lengthen our life span by as much as five years. At university, you will have many opportunities to build a social community around you.

9   Privacy

As well as needing time with others, we need time to ourselves to process our own thoughts, consolidate our learning and reflect on our experiences.

10   Status in social groupings

We don't need to be at the top of every social group, but it helps to know what is expected of us, the role we play and how we fit in.

You can use this framework to audit yourself and identify any barriers that are preventing you from meeting your needs in balance. Perhaps, for instance, you need to develop your own skills and knowledge if you don't know how to meet some of these needs. Or perhaps something happened to you in the past that means you find it difficult to feel safe or in control. Or maybe you just need to make some practical changes in your life to meet your needs in better balance.

Or maybe you're already doing a good job of meeting your needs and that's why you feel good right now.

Whatever is happening, paying attention to what is going on in your life can be a first step to either improving or maintaining your wellbeing. On page 14, you can find an audit template to help you do this. Remember, the key is to meet your needs in balance – if you are not meeting one of your needs or you are meeting it too much (having too much fun, for example), then it may have a negative impact on your wellbeing.

It's also important to bear in mind that, in real life, there is no perfect way of achieving balance. Trying to create perfect wellbeing is a trap that can undermine the way you feel and can rob you of the benefits of the good things you are already doing – believing that what you're doing isn't good enough can mean you ignore what is going well and focus just on what you think you aren't doing well enough.

Instead, focus on finding small practical steps that can help you improve how well you are meeting your needs right now and celebrate those steps – any improvement, no matter how small, is a real improvement.

When completing the audit template, consider how well you've been meeting your needs within the last two weeks. For each need, you will see there is a spectrum with a point of balance in the middle. By ticking the corresponding box beneath the descriptions, indicate on the audit where on each spectrum you would place yourself.

Once you have done this for each need, review what you have indicated. If a tick is towards the middle (in boxes 3–5), then you are meeting this need reasonably well. If you are towards one of the two ends (1–2 or 6–7), then you may benefit from thinking

How often do you feel safe and secure?

I never feel safe.   I always feel safe   I regularly take large risks
                               and secure.   that make me unsafe.

←——→

How often do you feel in control of your life and decisions?

I never feel in control.   I feel mostly in control and   I have to be in control
                               sometimes comfortable letting   at all times or I
                               others take control.   feel distressed.

←——→

How often do you feel good at something or that you are making a valuable contribution?

I never feel good at   I regularly feel competent and   I only do things I know I can
    anything.   confident in my abilities and challenge   do well and avoid doing
                           myself to try out new things.   anything I can't.

←——→

How much of your time is spent on things you find meaningful?

Nothing in my life feels   Most of my time is spent on   I refuse to do things that
    meaningful.   meaningful things and I try to   have no meaning to me even
                            find meaning in anything   if they're important to others
                            else that I'm required to do.   or refusing has negative
                                                                consequences for me.

←——→

How much of your time is spent on having fun?

I never have any fun.   I have a good balance of fun,   I spend all of my time having
                               rest and work.   fun and no time on other things.

←——→

How often do you feel you get the attention that you need from others?

Never – I feel invisible and   I feel comfortable with the   I feel uncomfortable and
    ignored.   amount of attention I get   overwhelmed by the amount
                              from others.   of attention I receive.

←——→

How often do you feel emotionally and intimately connected with at least one other person?

I never feel emotionally and   I regularly feel emotionally   I constantly create situations
intimately connected to with   connected to at least one   that generate emotional
    anyone.   other person and am   connections and feel abandoned
                              satisfied.   without onstant reassurance.

←——→

How often do you feel part of a wider community?

Never – I feel isolated.   I feel part of at least one community   I feel part of a community but
                               and have a comfortable sense of   feel my own identity and needs
                               belonging.   get completely lost within it.

←——→

How often do you get privacy, time and space to yourself?

I never get any space or avoid   I get a comfortable amount of   I'm always on my own.
spending any time alone.   time to myself.

←——→

Do you feel your status is recognised by others in the groups you're a part of?

No, I'm not appreciated at all.   My status is appropriately   I feel that people expect far too
                                  recognised.   much from me.

←——→

about practical changes you might make to your day-to-day life to move this more towards the middle. If you find this difficult or there are some barriers in the way, then it may be worth accessing some further support.

Meeting your needs as a student

Student life can make it both easier and more difficult to meet your needs in balance.

For instance, many students find that going to university can move them away from the social support and networks that they already have in place. This makes it more difficult for them to meet their need for attention, a sense of community and emotional intimacy. However, universities also offer lots of opportunities to meet new and like-minded people and to be part of a new community.

Being aware of your needs and trying to positively use the advantages of being a student can make a real difference to how you feel.

Other models of wellbeing

Although thinking about innate needs helps a lot of people, as we have already said, nothing works for everyone. Thankfully, there are other models out there that you may find more helpful – although you may also notice some overlaps between all of these models. Here are two more models that you might like to explore further.

Five ways to wellbeing – New Economics Foundation

Considering a range of emerging evidence from the field of psychology, the New Economics Foundation identified five practical elements to maintaining wellbeing [9]:

Connect...	Building and maintaining social connections throughout your life boost your wellbeing.
Be active...	Staying physically healthy and pursuing exercise, by doing something you enjoy, improve your physical and psychological health.
Take notice...	Being curious and mindful about the world around you, looking up from your phone and

paying attention to nature, people, your surroundings and yourself can make you feel more connected, grounded and in control.

Keep learning...   Learning is good for us, and as a student, you are already surrounded by new learning opportunities. Learning can expand our sense of purpose, help us achieve new wisdom, and be fun.

Give...   Helping others is good for us – it connects us to community and helps us to look outside our own thoughts.

The PERMA route to flourishing – Martin Seligman

Martin Seligman is one of the founders of Positive Psychology, which is the study of what it takes to live a happy, pleasant, engaged and meaningful life. Pulling together his work in this area, he devised a model that goes by the acronym PERMA [10], which stands for

Positive emotion   Regularly experiencing positive emotions like pleasure and holding positive views – being optimistic – can alter how you feel and how much you can do. Finding pleasure in difficult tasks (e.g., enjoying challenging academic tasks) can be particularly beneficial.

Engagement   Taking part in activities that absorb our full attention, so that we enter a state called 'flow', can improve not only our wellbeing but also our learning, creativity and performance – we'll discuss this more in Chapter 4.

Relationships   As we have already seen, we are social animals and we need relationships to thrive.

Meaning   Having a larger focus that gives us meaning and purpose can help us to feel more connected, motivated and satisfied.

Accomplishments   Achieving things that are important to us can help us to feel competent and in control of our lives – it helps if the things you are achieving are also connected to the things that give you meaning.

Further reading

Models of wellbeing

Fletcher, G. (2016). *The Philosophy of Wellbeing: An Introduction.* Abingdon: Routledge.

Griffin, J. & Tyrrell, I. (2003). *Human Givens: A New Approach to Emotional Health and Clear Thinking.* Chalvington: HG Press.

New Economics Foundation. (2008). *Five Ways to Wellbeing.* London: NEF.

Seligman, M. (2011). *Flourish: A New Understanding of Happiness and Well-Being – And How to Achieve Them.* London: Nicholas Brearley Publishing.

Living a happy/flourishing life

Aristotle. (2011). Aristotle's *Nicomachean Ethics.* (trans.) R. C. Bartlett & S. D. Collins. Chicago: Chicago University Press.

Ben-Shahar, T. (2008). *Happier.* London: McGraw Hill – The Observers.

Dolan, P. (2015). *Happiness by Design.* London: Penguin.

Layard, R. (2006). *Happiness.* London: Penguin.

References

1   Plato. (2007). *Plato's Complete Works.* M. Lane (Ed.). H. D. P. Lee & D. Lee. (trans.). London: Penguin Classics.

2   Aristotle. (2011). Aristotle's *Nicomachean Ethics.* (trans.) R. C. Bartlett & S. D. Collins. Chicago: Chicago University Press.

3   De Bruyckere, P., Kirchner, P. A. & Hulshof, C. D. (2015). *Urban Myths About Learning and Education.* Oxford: Elsevier Academic Press.

4   Glasser, W. (1985). *Control Theory: A New Explanation for How We Control Our Lives.* London: Harper & Row.

5   Lazarus, A. (1997). *Brief But Comprehensive Psychotherapy.* New York: Springer Publishing.

6   Deci, E. L. & Ryan, R. M. (1985). *Intrinsic Motivation and Self-Determination in Human Behavior.* New York: Plenum Publishing Co.

7   Fletcher, G. (2016). Objective List Theories. In: G. Fletcher (Ed.), *The Philosophy of Wellbeing: An Introduction.* Abingdon: Routledge.

8   Griffin, J. & Tyrrell, I. (2003). *Human Givens: A New Approach to Emotional Health and Clear Thinking.* Chalvington: HG Press.

9   New Economics Foundation. (2008). *Five Ways to Wellbeing.* London: NEF.

10 Seligman, M. (2011). *Flourish: A New Understanding of Happiness and Well-Being – And How to Achieve Them.* London: Nicholas Brearley Publishing.

Improve your wellbeing to improve your learning

3

Have you ever had any of the following experiences?

1 You were feeling nervous while studying for an exam and suddenly realised you'd just read the same page three times without taking in a single word.

2 You studied and prepared really well for an exam, turned over the paper to begin and realised that you couldn't remember a single thing you'd revised.

3 You spotted someone whom you found very attractive and you wanted to get to know them better, went up to speak to them and then realised that you couldn't speak actual words.

All of these things are examples of what we call 'emotional hijacking'. What this means is that the thinking part of your brain has been hijacked by the emotional part. It's completely normal and something we all experience from time to time. We even know how it works.

Let's talk about your brain

It seems obvious to say it, but all of the learning and academic work that you do takes place in your brain. Being a student is actually a bit like being a high-performance athlete – you are using part of your body (your brain) to perform to a high performance level. In fact, you are using the most powerful part of your body; your brain uses one fifth of all of the calories you burn over a typical day.

ASKHAM BRYAN
COLLEGE
LEARNING RESOURCES

For that reason, it's important that you look after your brain so that it can look after you. In this chapter, we're going to talk about some ways you can do that and how that might help both your wellbeing and learning.

We're going to start by examining emotional hijacking and the way in which your emotions can have both positive and negative impacts on the quality of your learning and performance.

Emotional hijacking

You probably already know that your brain is incredibly complex. Your brain is responsible for remembering and co-ordinating your relationships with other people, problem-solving, remembering the new material you've been learning, moving you around, letting you know that you have to pee and hundreds of other things, many of them at the same time and without your noticing. To do this, it co-ordinates intricate networks between the different parts of your brain, evaluating what is most important now and making decisions about what you should do next.

One of the parts of our brain is called the amygdala – we actually have two of them, one on each side of our brain. They're tiny little almond-shaped things, and they play a number of crucial roles, one of which is to trigger our fear circuit whenever we're in danger [1].

The easiest way to think about the amygdala is to imagine it as your brain's security officer [2]. When it picks up that you might be at risk, it starts a process called the fight-flight-freeze response. It doesn't matter whether the risk is physical, emotional or social or whether the evidence for the risk is in the real world or just in your thoughts; the same mechanism kicks in.

The fight-flight-freeze response has a number of immediate physical effects: it sends blood pumping to our muscles, it heightens our senses and we start to breathe in extra oxygen. It's basically preparing us to run away quickly from whatever the dangerous thing is, fight it off or freeze, so that it doesn't notice us or assumes we're already dead and not worth bothering with.

But it does another interesting thing. To the degree that it picks up risk, our brain's security officer sends cascading chemical signals into the part of your brain that is most involved in complex thought: the dorsolateral prefrontal cortex. It's a part that is crucial for academic learning – and the security officer switches it off [1].

That's why you go completely blank in the exam. The security officer has picked up on your anxious thoughts and feelings, decided that you must be in danger and triggered a fight-flight-freeze response.

Now, why does this happen – why do we have one part of our brain that can switch off another? The lead researcher who identified this process, Joseph LeDoux, provides a useful example of why this process can at times be useful [1]. Imagine you are in a country where poisonous snakes are common. You are out walking in the wild, and suddenly just in front of you, you see a shape – it might be a poisonous snake or it might just be a stick that looks a bit like a snake.

In a situation like this, you don't want the academic part of your brain to get involved. In brain-processing terms, it's actually very slow and it's also going to want to complicate things with questions like – are you a stick or a snake? Are you a poisonous snake? Just how poisonous are you? Have you noticed me? – by which time the snake will have bitten you and the poison will be flowing through your bloodstream.

So, instead, the security officer takes charge, tells the academic part of your brain to be quiet and orders your body to jump back. If it's a stick, you might feel a bit silly; but you're still alive. If it was a poisonous snake, then it just saved your life.

As you can see, this is actually an excellent system for keeping you safe in a dangerous situation. It's fantastic if you've just walked in front of a snake – it just happens to be absolutely rubbish if you're trying to sit an exam.

Resetting your system

There are a number of techniques and strategies that you can use to get your brain working again if you find yourself in this situation. Try experimenting with and combining some of these suggestions:

1 First, if at all possible, stop whatever it is you are trying to do. If you're doing an exam, put your pen down. If you're working at home, get up from your desk. Trying to force yourself to keep working will only make you more frustrated and anxious right now. Some people find it helps to imagine a stop sign in their mind or to say 'stop' out loud if possible.

2 Accept that you feel anxious. Remember, negative emotions are trying to help us and keep us safe. (We'll discuss this a bit more later on in this chapter.) Try to avoid arguing with the anxiety or telling yourself that you 'shouldn't' feel this way or 'should' be able to cope. Just remind yourself that it's ok to be anxious and that you are safe.

3 Breathe – many people find that breathing techniques can be the quickest and easiest way to calm down and reset their system. (See '7/11 breathing' below.)

4 Notice and accept the physical sensation. Sometimes, just noticing that this is just a physical feeling and focussing upon it can be enough to make it dissipate.

5 Change your environment. Moving can break the emotional trance – if you're inside, go outdoors. If you're outside, move back indoors. If you are in an exam, you can ask the invigilator for a toilet break.

6 Notice your surroundings in detail – focussing on a patch of colour, the movement of a tree or a spot on the wall and picking out as many details about it as you can may help your brain to refocus and calm down.

7 Once you are calm, think about what you want to write, say or do next and then restart whatever you were doing.

7/11 breathing

There are a number of breathing techniques that people find helpful, but this is the one I like most [2]. I've taught this technique to thousands of students over the years, and I regularly get feedback that it is the most useful thing I teach. It becomes more effective the more you do it and can reduce tension that you might not even have noticed. If you can practice it for a few minutes a few times a day, you might find that it helps you feel calmer generally and quickly reduces anxiety when it strikes. As we move through the book, I've also included a few alternative relaxation exercises.

- We call this 7/11 breathing because you breathe in for 7 and out for 11.
- If there is ever a time when breathing for that long isn't possible, it doesn't matter. As long as the out-breath is much longer than the in-breath, it will still work. We call it 7/11 because it sounds like the shop, so people are more likely to remember it.
- The key to this technique is to aim the breath deep into your stomach. It might help if you put your hands on your stomach so you can feel it swelling up as you breathe in.
- Allow your lungs to empty and then breathe deeply into your stomach while counting to 7.
- Once you reach 7, breathe out gently to the count of 11.
- Repeat this for 2 to 3 minutes or until you feel calm and relaxed.

Negative emotions are ok

Feeling anxious, angry, lonely or sad can be painful and unpleasant. But that doesn't mean that negative emotions are always bad or should always be avoided. Like all of our emotions, negative emotions are doing a job – they are motivating you to take action so that you can be safe and thrive, now and in the future.

Fear emotions, like anxiety and anger, can help to keep us safe in dangerous situations. Loneliness can motivate us to seek out more social connections. Feeling upset brings your attention to the fact that something isn't right in your life or that something bad has happened and that you may need to make changes, adapt to new circumstances or focus your attention on looking after yourself for a while.

Listening to your negative emotions and what they are trying to tell you can often be helpful. In contrast, trying to ignore how you feel or push away negative feelings and thoughts can make them last longer. There is a general rule in psychology that what we resist, persists and amplifies. (If you don't believe me, try not to think about pink socks. Really. Try very hard not to picture pink socks in your mind. Don't think about pink socks. Do not picture pink socks in your mind. Many of you are now thinking about pink socks!)

If we try to fight negative emotions, we tend to become anxious about the fact that we're anxious, depressed about feeling depressed or angry about feeling angry. In doing so, we've doubled the negative feelings. Instead, listen to what the emotion is trying to tell you and then see if there are some positive actions you can take to deal with whatever is causing the feeling.

Of course, sometimes our negative emotions can react in ways that aren't helpful. They misread situations and motivate us to do things that aren't good for us. For instance, they mistake an exam for a dangerous situation and make us want to run out of the door to escape from it – which would result in our failing the exam. At this point, they are no longer functioning as they should – which is why we sometimes refer to them as dysfunctional.

Learning to tell the difference between functional and dysfunctional negative emotions can help you to take control, make good decisions and feel better. This is a skill that you can develop – throughout the book, we'll discuss ways you can do this. To begin with, just focus on becoming aware of your emotions, what they are trying to motivate you to do and whether or not this is actually helpful for you.

The impact of stress on academic learning

There is a myth that I sometimes encounter when working with students. It goes something like this: 'If I'm taking my studies seriously, I should be stressed. Working hard and being stressed go hand in hand; I should expect to be stressed. All students are stressed and if they aren't it's because they don't care enough and are probably going to fail'.

This myth is particularly prevalent among post-graduate students but it's increasingly common amongst under-grads too. Why do I call it a myth? Well, because it isn't true.

As we've already discussed in this chapter, emotional hijacking reduces your ability to think, learn and solve complex problems. Being stressed is a form of emotional hijacking. Again, stress itself isn't bad but it's a short-term fear emotion. A short burst of stress when you need some motivation to act can be useful. Feeling stressed for prolonged periods of time, without the chance to recover, is not helpful. Prolonged stress is particularly not good for academic learning or performance.

However, being stretched is good for learning and performance. When we are stretched, we find the situation that we are in challenging and difficult and we may feel pushed to the limits of our abilities but believe that we can succeed. Being stretched is good for us generally – it helps us feel that life has meaning and purpose and it strengthens us emotionally, making us more able to respond in a healthy way to challenging circumstances in the future. This is why some people talk about regular bouts of stretch as a form of stress inoculation.

Although stress and stretch are different in effect overall, physically they can feel very similar – both speed up our heart rate and both can give us butterflies in the stomach. This is why you might hear people talk about 'good stress'; they are confusing stretch for stress.

Stress vs. stretch

So what is the difference between stress and stretch?

Stress, as we've already discussed, is a fear response. It can reduce your thinking ability, lower your mood, leave you feeling that you have little control and time, reduce your energy and negatively impact on performance.

Stretch, on the other hand, uses a completely different neurological circuit that improves our thinking and helps us make more connections and think creative thoughts. When we are stretched, we feel challenged and may well find some things difficult but we also feel motivated and in control and believe we can be successful.

We often feel at our best when we've taken on a difficult task and, with hard work, completed it successfully. It's one of the reasons that learning is so good for us – learning new things stretches us. Boredom and a lack of purpose, on the other hand, can be bad for our wellbeing. When we discussed our emotional needs in the previous chapter, we looked at the importance of balance. Being stretched is the optimum point of balance between boredom and stress.

Feeling stretched	Feeling stressed
Feel challenged	Feel overwhelmed
Feel success is in your control	Feel success is out of your control
Feel supported	Feel abandoned
Feel motivated	Feel anxious/fearful
Improved performance	Mental freezing

Thinking creates reality

Paying attention to how we are feeling and trying to stay 'in stretch' can help us to feel healthier and more positive. It is also important to make the distinction between being stretched and stressed so that we don't talk ourselves into being stressed when we aren't. If we tell ourselves that we are stressed – then we usually do become stressed, even if we weren't before.

For human beings, our thoughts really do create reality – this is something we've known since the time of Confucius. The world is too big and too complicated for us to perceive and understand it all at once; So our brain filters the world for us, allowing us to focus on what is important. It decides what is important by using the thoughts, narratives and stories we already have in our heads. In this way, our thinking creates the world and our experience of it.

If you want to test this out, here's a little experiment I often run in classrooms. I'm not sure where it originally came from, but my colleague Sarah Williams shared it with me. It's a fascinating and fun thing to do and I'd recommend that you try it out with your friends and family.

First, imagine that you have a lemon in one hand and a knife in the other. Focus on the lemon. Imagine what it feels like in your hand, feel the weight of it. Feel the skin of the lemon against the skin of your hand. Feel the curve of its shape. Now look down at the lemon. Imagine the yellow colour of its skin, see the pimples and shape. Hold the lemon up to your nose and breathe in that lemony smell.

Now take the knife and cut the lemon in half. Concentrate on one of the halves. Look at the yellow flesh inside. See the juice bubbling up to the top. Lift it up and smell how much stronger that lemony smell is now.

Now lean forward and bite into the lemon.

Did your mouth just twist a little? Or did your face completely contort at the thought of the sharp lemon juice? Even if you didn't react, you may find that you are salivating a little more. When I do this in groups, usually about a third of people react strongly and some refuse to even imagine biting a lemon.

And yet there is no lemon there.

We experience this phenomenon at other times as well. For instance, when watching a horror film, we can be absolutely terrified even though the film poses no actual threat to us. We could turn off the TV or leave the cinema, and the scary images and story would stop. The evil monster can't actually get at us and it isn't real – but our imagination makes us think it is really happening, and so we are scared.

That's why it's important to be aware of whether your own thoughts are helping you. If you tell yourself that being a student is going to be stressful or that you won't cope, then that belief will make you feel stressed and overwhelmed. If, on the other hand, you are able to say – this is stretching and at times I'm going to find this difficult but if I work hard and look after myself sensibly, I think I can to do it – then you reduce your emotional arousal, free up more of your academic brain power and give yourself the chance of performing to your ability.

When anxiety wants to make you stressed

Of course, it isn't always that easy to change our thoughts. Anxiety can hijack our imagination, convincing us that the situation we are in is stressful or awful or that dire things await us in our future. At times like these, it can be difficult to work out what is a real problem that needs your attention and what is an imagined worry that isn't helping.

The easiest way to think about anxiety is to imagine it as being a bit like a parasite. It gets into your system and convinces you that it's part of you, so you start to think 'I'm just a naturally anxious person' or 'I'm a worrier'. Then it manipulates you to behave and think in ways that feed and make the anxiety stronger and make you weaker.

For instance, let's imagine that you have a tricky assignment that you're a little bit nervous about. Starting it early and working hard on it will make it more likely that you will complete a quality piece of work on time and the nervousness will disappear. So instead, anxiety will raise your stress levels and persuade you to avoid the assignment and pretend it doesn't exist. You hide it in the corner of your room and absorb yourself in social media or binging on a box set. As a result, when the deadline gets closer, you feel three times more anxious than you would have if you'd started the assignment on time.

Working with anxious thoughts

Begin by simply identifying when it's you thinking and when it's anxiety thinking. Sometimes, you might be aware of two thought processes running in your head: one trying to make you anxious, the other recognising that there is no need to be anxious now. One is anxiety, the other is you.

- If you can't spot anxiety thinking when it is happening, don't worry. This is a skill that you can improve, and most people need practice to be able to do it well. When you start trying to build this skill, you might realise only after the event that you've been hijacked by anxiety. Then you might start to realise that you're experiencing anxiety in the moment but not be able to do anything about it. Finally, you will begin to recognise the early signs of anxiety and be able to interrupt them and take control before anxiety can take charge. Be patient with yourself and for now just focus on building your awareness of anxiety and how it manipulates you.

- Don't argue with anxiety. It has access to your imagination and will come up with compelling reasons to convince you that you are wrong – even if they are nonsense. I often say that you should treat anxiety like a child having a tantrum. If you try to logically explain to the child why they shouldn't be having a tantrum, generally the tantrum just gets worse. Simply notice the anxiety, accept it, breathe and then move your mind away from it. For example, focus on your breathing or on something in nature or music or the feel of your feet on the floor or on a fun or creative thought.

- Be curious – notice how anxiety reacts to you and what it tries to do next, and notice that you don't have to obey its instructions.

  Some people find it helpful to work with the thoughts to show that they are nonsense (without arguing with them). For instance, you might want to take control of the thoughts and exaggerate them to make fun of them.

- Keep breathing – using 7/11 breathing can help to keep you calm and focus your mind (see page 23).

- Remember what it is that you wanted to do – what is the anxiety trying to persuade you to avoid? When you feel calmer, do what you wanted to do – don't let the anxiety stop you.

- If you don't succeed in taking control this time, don't let anxiety use that as a weapon against you ('See you failed, so what was the point?', etc.). The fact that you tried means that you've practised, and what we practise we get good at. Managing anxiety can be a tricky skill – you wouldn't expect to be able to play a musical instrument straight away, but the more you practise the more it becomes second nature.

Progressive muscle relaxation

This is another relaxation exercise that you can use instead of or alongside 7/11 breathing. Again, practicing will make this work more effectively. Don't worry if it doesn't work for you straight away; try to do it for a few days in a row and see if it gets easier each time.

- Find a quiet comfortable place to sit, where you can relax.

- Start with one foot and tense it up as tight as you possibly can – try not to tense the muscles around your foot. Push all of your tension into that one tensed-up area – this may feel uncomfortable for a moment or two.

- Quickly release the tensed muscles and let them relax as much as possible. Pay close attention as the feeling of relaxation flows into the muscles. Notice how this feels and how different it is from tension.

- Take a moment or two for that area to relax and then turn your attention to the lower half of your leg and repeat the exercise – tense, then relax.

- Keep working up your leg until you reach your waist and then do the same with your other leg. Then work up your body and down each arm into your hands.

- Remember to take time after you relax each area to focus on how it feels and how much more relaxed it is now.

Physical wellbeing

Your physical wellbeing can also have a significant impact on both your learning and your psychological wellbeing. Exercise, diet, hydration, sleep, sunlight and being close to nature have all been shown to affect academic performance and your overall wellbeing. (See the box on page 35 for some of the evidence that demonstrates this.) But in my work with students, the one that concerns me most is sleep.

Sleep, learning and wellbeing

When I'm in front of a class of students, I usually ask for a show of hands in response to the question, 'Are you regularly getting a good night's sleep?' On average, out of about 20 students, two or three hands go up. Of course, this is very unscientific, but research does suggest that many students are experiencing poor sleep [3]. More concerning still, many of the students I talk to view poor sleep as a normal fact of life that they should just accept. As researchers such as Matthew Walker have pointed out, not getting enough sleep increases the likelihood of getting ill (mentally and physically), impairs our judgement, causes weight gain and reduces our overall ability to perform [4].

Sleep plays a crucial role in maintaining our health, repairing our bodies and topping up our energy levels. Sleep has also been shown to have clear impacts on learning and performance – the quantity and quality of the sleep you get are closely related to your capacity to learn and your academic performance [5].

Our brain does three things in sleep that are vital to our learning:

1 The brain clears out unnecessary information that you've picked up over the course of the day. Think of it like deleting unneeded data to free up more memory space so you can learn more the next day [4].

2 The important things we've learned get moved into our long-term memory while we're asleep. If we don't sleep well, we are more likely to forget the things we've learned [6].

3   We problem-solve when we are asleep. If you are set a difficult problem that you can't solve at the first attempt, you will be more likely to solve it at the second attempt if you've been to sleep in between [7].

If you are a music student or your studies involve any kind of physical skill development, this also beds in while we are asleep. If a piano player is struggling to play a difficult piece, they will be more likely to be able to play it after they've had a good night's sleep [4].

Sleeping improves exam performance more than cramming

Studies have repeatedly shown that giving up sleep in order to cram for an exam results in lower grades. Yes, you read that right. Extra revision can reduce your performance on an exam – if you give up sleep. For instance, in one study [8], students' sleep was monitored in the week before their exams. Students who slept more than 8 hours a night outperformed those who slept 7.9 hours or less. In fact, sleeping more was associated with a four-point grade boost.

How much sleep do we need?

On average, adults need 8 to 8.5 hours of sleep per night. Ignore newspaper articles that tell you most people need only 6 hours a night or that high performers sleep less than other people. This simply isn't borne out by the evidence.

As with most things related to humans, the amount of sleep we each need will be slightly different and there does appear to be a spectrum. However, the number of people who actually thrive on 6 hours a night is very small – so small that you are not in that group. The problem is that when people are sleep-deprived, they often don't know that they are sleep deprived – they normalise the impacts of sleeplessness and don't notice the negative effects. But the negative effects are still there and they will cause long-term problems for your health and reduce your academic performance [4].

Aim for 8 hours a night and give yourself the opportunity to get the sleep you need. Even if you aren't asleep for the whole time, being relaxed and away from wakeful activity will have benefits, and you increase the likelihood that you will sleep well.

The key thing to remember is that for most people, if you don't currently sleep well, it is absolutely possible to improve your sleep (unless there is a physical problem that is disrupting your sleep). It is very easy for our sleep cycles to get out of sync – especially if you've moved away from home and are sleeping in a new environment like a hall of residence or dorm. Don't assume that sleeplessness is just something you are stuck with – try some of the tips below and give them time to work. (If you can maintain some of these tips for a few weeks, they usually do.) If after that you are still experiencing problems, then speak to your doctor or a counsellor for some help.

Tips for improving your sleep

- What you do in the day affects your sleep. Having a good routine and structure in your day helps your brain to understand when it is daytime (and you should be awake) and when it is nighttime (and you should be asleep). Being active also helps to tire you out. Try to eat regularly across the day – including breakfast within an hour of waking up.
- Get out into the sun; 20 to 30 minutes of sunlight each day helps your brain to calibrate wake time and sleep time.
- Exercising regularly has been shown to improve sleep overall. This doesn't have to mean going to the gym; going for a walk can be equally helpful.

- Reduce caffeine – caffeine has a half-life of 8 hours and blocks receptors that allow you to sleep. Try not to drink caffeine after midday.

- Try not to work on your bed – it can be difficult in student accommodation because there may not be much space in your room, but if you can, avoid doing wakeful activity like working or watching TV on your bed. Allow your brain to pair your bed with going to sleep.

- No screens at least 1 hour before bed. Switch off your phone and iPad and laptop – even if it does have a blue light filter, it is still light. Buy an alarm clock instead of using your phone, and let your friends know that you will not respond to messages at night.

- Use the last hour to create a pre-sleep routine that relaxes you and primes your brain and body for sleep. You can read, listen to music, have a bath or shower, meditate, draw, use relaxing scents, take off make-up and so on. If you wear pyjamas to bed, don't put them on until this last hour.

- Put unwanted thoughts in a box. We are more vulnerable to racing or anxious thoughts just before we fall asleep, but this is also a really bad time to problem-solve. If you try not to think about these thoughts, you will think about them more. So instead, promise to think about them later. Some people like to write the thoughts down; others like to imagine locking them away in a box. Revisit them in the morning to see whether they need your attention.

- If you are still awake after 20 minutes or so, get back up and do something necessary but dull. I normally recommend reading the dullest textbook you've got while standing up. After a few minutes, you'll probably find yourself nodding off and you can get back into bed. If you wake up again, simply repeat until your brain gets the message and lets you sleep.

Improving your physical wellbeing to improve your academic learning and performance

As we have already discussed, when trying to make improvements to any aspect of your life, start with achievable steps that feel positive and possible. Be wary of people who say things like 'if you aren't exercising for x hours week, then there is no point'. This is nonsense. One hour of exercise is obviously better than none. In fact, some research suggests that just getting up from your desk and moving about more during the day can deliver benefits to your health and performance.

If you want to improve your physical wellbeing, start with one or two small steps that you think you can fit into your life right now. Remember, we're just going for an improvement, not perfection: eating a little healthier, getting a bit more exercise, getting into the sunlight a little more often. Simple changes can help you do this, such as having fruit in your bag to snack on instead of chocolate, carrying a water bottle you can top up, taking longer routes to class or using stairs if you can and travelling around the outside of a building rather than through it. Once you've embedded that change into your daily routine, you take the next achievable step and improve again.

Some students find that it can be helpful to team up with their friends and commit to making improvements together. Sharing the steps in this way means you are also meeting some of your social needs.

Remember to mark and congratulate yourself for any improvements you make. Feeling that you are making progress makes it easier to keep going.

Physical wellbeing, your mood and your learning – what does the research tell us?

Diet

There is a clear and well-evidenced link between food and mood. If you live on caffeine, sugar and high-fat foods, you are more likely to experience anxiety and low mood [9, 10]. A healthy diet can help you to feel emotionally better. Research has also shown that a healthy diet improves concentration, memory and academic performance [11] but that a diet high in sugar and fat can impair memory and cognitive functioning [12]. It is equally important to eat regularly throughout the day – going into a lecture hungry will reduce the amount you learn.

Hydration

A report to the British Psychological Society Conference demonstrated that hydration can have an effect on exam performance. Just by staying hydrated during an exam, some students were shown to have boosted their performance by up to 10% [13]. So arriving at an exam already hydrated and staying hydrated during it might help your performance.

Exercise

Exercise can be more effective at managing anxiety and low mood than medication [14]. It has also been shown to improve concentration, creativity, learning and academic performance [15].

Sunlight

Studies have shown that access to sunlight can have a significant impact on learning and performance. Children in classrooms with external windows were found to outperform those in classrooms with no windows [16]. Not getting enough sunlight can also lead to depression and loss of motivation.

Further reading

Improving wellbeing

Duhigg, C. (2013). *The Power of Habit.* London: Random House.

Joseph, K. & Irons, C. (2018). *Managing Stress.* London: Red Globe Press.

Walker, M. (2017). *Why We Sleep.* London: Penguin Books.

The brain, emotions and human behaviour

Kahneman, D. (2012). *Thinking Fast and Slow.* London: Penguin.

LeDoux, J. (1998) *The Emotional Brain.* London: Phoenix.

Mischel, W. (2014). *The Marshmallow Test.* London: Corgi.

References

1   LeDoux, J. (1998). *The Emotional Brain.* London: Phoenix.
2   Griffin, J. & Tyrrell, I. (2003). *Human Givens: A New Approach to Emotional Health and Clear Thinking.* Chalvington: HG Press.
3   Becker, S. P., Jarrett, M. A., Luebbe, A. M., Garner, A. A., Burns, G. L. & Kofler, M. J. (2018). Sleep in a Large, Multi-university Sample of College Students: Sleep Problem Prevalence, Sex Differences, and Mental Health Correlates. *Sleep Health: Journal of the National Sleep Foundation,* 4(2), 174–181.
4   Walker, M. (2017). *Why We Sleep.* London: Penguin Books.
5   Curcio, G., Ferrara, M. & De Gennaro, L. (2006). Sleep Loss, Learning Capacity and Academic Performance. *Sleep Medicine Reviews,* 10, 232–337.
6   Stickgold, R. (2005). Sleep-Dependent Memory Consolidation. *Nature,* 437, 1272–1278.
7   Sio, U. N., Monaghan, P. & Ormerod, T. (2013). Sleep on It, but Only If It Is Difficult: Effects of Sleep on Problem Solving. *Memory & cognition,* 41(2), 159–166.
8   Scullin, M. K. (2019). The Eight Hour Sleep Challenge During Final Exams Week. *Teaching of Psychology,* 46(1), 55–63.
9   Rogers, P. J. (2001). A Healthy Body, a Healthy Mind: Long-Term Impact of Diet on Mood and Cognitive Function. *Proceedings of the Nutrition Society,* 60(1), 135–143.
10 Francis, H. M., Stevenson, R. J., Chambers, J. R., Gupta, D., Newey, B. & Lim, C. K. (2019). A Brief Diet Intervention Can Reduce Symptoms of Depression in Young Adults – A Randomised Controlled Trial. *PLoS ONE,* 14(10), e0222768.

11 Florence, M. D., Asbridge, M. & Veugelers, P. J. (2008). Diet Quality and Academic Performance. *The Journal of School Health*, 78(4), 209–215.

12 Stevenson, R. J., Francis Heather, M., Attuquayefio, T., Gupta, D., Yeomans, M. R., Oaten, M. J. & Davidson, T. (2020). Hippocampal-Dependent Appetitive Control Is Impaired by Experimental Exposure to a Western-Style Diet. *Royal Society Open Science*, 7(2). doi:https://doi.org/10.1098/rsos.191338.

13 Pawson, C., Gardner, M., Doherty, S., Martin, L., Soares, R. & Edmonds, C. J. (2012). Water Consumption in Exams and Its Effects on Students' Performance. *Annual British Psychological Society Conference*, London 18–20 April.

14 Archer, T. (2016). Physical Exercise and Its Impact on Psychology. *Clinical and Experimental Psychology*, 2, 2.

15 Rasberry, C. N., Lee, S. M., Robin, L., Laris, B. A., Russell, L. A., Coyle, K. K. & Nihiser, A. J. (2011). The Association Between School-Based Physical Activity, Including Physical Education, and Academic Performance: A Systematic Review of the Literature. *Preventive Medicine*, 52, S10–S20.

16 Heschong, L., Wright, R. L. & Okura, S. (2002). Daylighting Impacts on Human Performance in School. *Journal of the Illuminating Engineering Society.*, 31(2), 101–104.

Improve your learning to improve your wellbeing

So far, we've looked at ways in which your wellbeing can impact on your learning. But, as we mentioned in Chapter 1, your learning and academic performance can also influence your wellbeing. The relationship between learning and wellbeing is 'transactional' – it moves in both directions.

There are generally three main processes through which learning can impact on your wellbeing:

1 **The way in which you engage psychologically with your learning**
How you think about learning – whether you focus on learning or grades – and how emotionally engaged you become with the subject have been shown to have a relationship with your emotional wellbeing and levels of satisfaction.

2 **Your mastery and skill level**
Feeling competent and capable and being able to tackle difficult problems with confidence can help you to develop a sense of 'mastery'. This supports motivation and self-belief and leads to better emotional wellbeing.

3 **Assessment grades and the value you place on achievement**
Unsurprisingly, good grades can improve how we feel and bad grades can lower our mood and undermine our confidence – at least in the short term. We'll talk more about how our response to lower grades can actually be beneficial, in the long term, in Chapter 11.

In this chapter, we'll take a look at these processes and identify ways in which you can take control of your learning to benefit your wellbeing and your academic performance.

Deep vs. surface learning

What do you focus on when you are completing an assessed piece of work?

Is your focus on using the piece of work to learn as much as you can about the subject? Or on trying to craft something that you feel proud of and passionate about, regardless of the grade you get? Or on trying to come up with a powerful argument for something you believe in? Or solve a problem in a way that might be beneficial for the world?

Or do you focus on getting the best grade possible? Or impressing your tutor? Or just getting the bare minimum done so you can pass this module or programme and move a step closer to finishing your degree?

Broadly speaking, these behaviours are associated with two different approaches to learning: deep and surface learning [1].

In deep learning, as the name suggests, you engage deeply with the subject, studying it because you are passionate about it and want to know more. You will read widely around the subject, think about it when you aren't in class or completing work, and talk to your friends about what you are learning. Your focus will be on improving your learning and your understanding so you can master your subject.

In surface learning, you skip over the surface of the subject, focussing only on what you need to know, to get the grade you want, in your assessments. You will read only as much as you need to and think little about your subject outside of class or study time. Your focus is on achieving the grade you want with the minimum amount of effort.

Deep learning	Surface learning
Reads and studies widely and deeply	Reads and studies narrowly
Aims to understand the meaning behind the material	Aims to regurgitate the material
Connects new material to previous knowledge and beliefs	Learns subjects in isolation
Seeks to create new arguments and ideas from what they have learned	Seeks to repeat arguments of others accurately
Motivated internally by desire to learn or love of subject	Externally motivated by the need to pass assessments or gain grades
Thinks critically about what they have learned	Focusses on memorising necessary material without examining it

Generally, most students combine these two approaches at different times, but as a whole, having a deeper learning approach is better for both your learning and your wellbeing.

Research has shown that students who take mainly a deep learning approach get better grades – ironically, focussing mainly on grades can cause you to perform below your ability [2]. Students with a deep learning approach also have better emotional wellbeing and tend to be more satisfied with their time at university overall.

Students who take a surface learning approach tend to get lower grades, be more prone to anxiety and burnout, and be less satisfied with their experience [3, 4].

From a psychological point of view, it is easy to see why these approaches may have a different impact on your wellbeing. Think back to the list of needs in Chapter 2 and in particular our need for control and for meaning and purpose.

The focus for deep learners is on learning and improving understanding – this is something that is largely within their control. If they improve their understanding and produce the piece of work that they want to produce, then they have remained in control of all of the elements that are important to them. Their learning is also a source of meaning (something we'll talk about more in the next chapter); as a result, they get a sense of pleasure and fulfilment from their academic work.

The focus for surface learners is on getting a grade. This is not something they can control – even if they produce a really good piece of work, it is the person who is marking it who will decide what grade it gets. The work also has no meaning beyond the grade and so the student will derive little pleasure and fulfilment from their studies. As a result, academic work can become something that induces anxiety or irritation (because you have to do something you don't enjoy or value) – if the grade is the only thing that matters and you aren't in control of the grade, then you might 'fail' on your own terms. In this way, the risk of failure can become a dominant thought.

Deep and surface learning lead to –

	Surface learning
Focus on subject	Focus on grades
High achievement	Lower achievement
Good wellbeing	Poor wellbeing (high anxiety)
More satisfied with teaching and learning	Less satisfied

Isn't some strategic learning beneficial for grades?

Of course, deep and surface approaches aren't the only ways of thinking about learning. An additional concern is whether your learning is organised or disorganised [4]. A deep learner who is disorganised might well get so lost in what they are doing that they forget to submit their work by the deadline.

It is also important to remember that surface learning is not always a bad thing. If you are on a module that you hate and can't find a way to care about it, if there are other things going on in your life that demand your focus and attention or if you are currently unwell, then taking a surface approach may be a very sensible and proper strategy. As always, finding the appropriate balance is key.

You can think about the combinations of deep/surface and organised/disorganised as set out in the table below; deep/organised provides the best learning, performance and wellbeing, and surface/disorganised provides the poorest learning performance and wellbeing.

	Deep learner/organised
• Minimum learning • Potential reasonable performance • Possible anxiety	• Maximum learning • High achievement • Good wellbeing
Surface learner/disorganised	**Deep learner/disorganised**
• Minimum learning • Underperformance • Anxiety and disappointment	• Significant learning • Potential underperformance • Potential disappointment

Moving from surface to deep learning

Unfortunately, many school systems around the world put a particular focus on end-of-school exam results and have moved increasingly towards training their students to take a surface learning approach. This means that you may not have been taught to learn deeply yet. That doesn't mean you can't be a deep learner. It just means that it's something you will need to learn to do – but that's ok. Learning is, after all, why we go to university. Let's look at some steps that might help.

1 Letting go of grades (a bit)

Of course, no one is going to claim that grades don't matter at all. If you fail all of your assessments, you are unlikely to finish university or feel very good about it. The key thing is whether grades are your main focus or whether they are secondary to your learning.

What we are really talking about is postponing the moment that you think about grades. You might think about the time frame between learning and grades like this:

- When you begin a new module or programme, try to focus on learning as much as you can about the subject, following elements that particularly interest you and reading and thinking widely.

● Then think about how you can bring that learning together with the assessment criteria you have been set. Because grades take so much of our attention, we often miss the fact that completing an assessed piece of work is actually a really good way to learn deeply. Having to work with new information helps to embed it in your memory. So, when you begin a new piece of work, try to focus on how you can use it to enhance your learning.

● Once you've pulled all of this together, you can think about how to maximise your grade (e.g., by ensuring you are meeting all of the assessment criteria).

2   Finding the emotional connection

It is easier to learn deeply if you are positively and emotionally engaged with your subject and if you are passionate or excited about or interested in the subject and believe it is important and meaningful. (That's why it's important to choose a degree subject that can light you up inside.)

However, it is not unusual for students to find that at least one subject on their course is less interesting to them – you may even find it boring or frustrating and see little point in studying it. It will be more difficult to learn deeply while you continue to feel like this – but that feeling doesn't necessarily have to stay the same. Sometimes, if we take the time to find an emotional connection with a subject, we can build new and more positive feelings about it.

Try the following exercise.

Pick one of the following deliberately dull topics:

● the brightness of street lights
● the history of socks
● finance and accounting in contemporary theatre

Now, try to come up with reasons why it is really important to study and understand this topic. It might take a while but take your time and consider what we might learn from studying these subjects – how might they effect real people or the world in some way? What might different politicians think about your topic?

If it helps, you may want to try this out with some friends or helpful family members.

I use this exercise in class and I always find it interesting to see how students go from looking at me with a slightly bemused expression and wondering what the point of the exercise is to arguing with each other about their chosen topic. (For examples of reasons that students have come up with for studying these subjects, see the end of the chapter.)

In fact, subjects that start off boring can often become a passion – let's look at a common example. Many psychology students don't like having to study statistics. A complaint I often hear is 'I want to study psychology because I care about people, not numbers'.

At face value, this seems like a fair response. What have numbers got to do with supporting people? However, in the field of mental health, statistics actually play a vital role in protecting real people. The way we can tell if a new treatment is helpful or harmful is by subjecting the outcomes of those treatments to statistical testing. That means statistics protect people from harm. In fact, statistics are a vital weapon against those who would seek to exploit the vulnerable by selling them harmful interventions. If you care about people, then you'll recognise that statistics are important and meaningful. (If you want to read more about this subject, I recommend *Bad Science* by Ben Goldacre [5].)

If you are studying a module or programme that you don't enjoy, try to find a way to connect with it emotionally. Look for reasons to care about it or some element of it. If it frustrates you or if you think that everything you hear your tutor say is wrong, see if you can find research or informed opinions that agree with you. If you can't find a way to care about the whole subject, can you find one part of it that might be a bit more interesting or engaging? Talk to your friends and see if they can provide you with reasons for caring about it. Or see if you can find a connection between this subject and another that you do care about.

3 Connect to other motivations

Sometimes, if the subject matter just won't engage you, it may be better to connect the subject you are studying to future plans you do care about. For instance, you might want to ask yourself the following:

- How will learning about this prepare me for the career I want? Will the knowledge or skills I acquire help me to perform better in my future role?

- How will learning about this help me to have the impact that I want to have on the world? Will it enable me to help others or come up with ways to improve things?

- How will learning about this help me to be a better student, so I can learn more and improve my performance?

- How will learning about this help me to meet my own goals?

This may help you to create positive associations with the subject and so make it easier to work on.

Alternatively, you can focus on how difficult it is to engage with this subject as an opportunity to develop the discipline and skill to work on things that you don't find interesting. In every career, there are things we don't enjoy but have to do – and often have to do well. Using boring subjects to experiment and finding ways to make hard work bearable will stand you in good stead for the future and it will make the time spent on the module or programme feel useful.

Write first with the heart, then with the head

The novelist Raymond Chandler said that the first draft should be written by the heart and the second by the head. You might like to try this when completing a written assignment, such as an essay. Use the first draft to write what you want to write. Make it your message to the world. In subsequent drafts, edit and make sure you are meeting assessment criteria. This combination will allow you to perform deeply and in an organised way.

When you begin an assignment, it can help to ask three questions:

1 **What am I being asked to do?**

What is the question? What does the marking brief say I should include? How long a piece of work is it?

2 **How should I go about completing this task?**

What's the best way to work on this? What resources do I need? What skills will I need to use? Do I need to brush up on any of those skills? Who can help? When am I best to work on it? Think about breaking the process down into chunks and timetable each stage (e.g., research, planning, first draft and second draft).

3 **Why do I care about this subject?**

What is it about this subject that makes me passionate, excited, angry, frustrated or interested? Is it possible to make the assignment about those things that emotionally resonate with me? Can I make this an assignment that is meaningful for me? Can I use it to suggest ways of righting wrongs, doing things better, creating new ideas or deepening my learning?

Meta-learning – learning about learning

Sometimes, when we adopt ineffective learning strategies, it is because we don't properly understand how learning actually happens.

It's not surprising that not knowing how something works can result in our adopting ineffective practices. Let me give you an example. I am old enough to remember when duvets and duvet covers replaced blankets and sheets on beds across the UK. Now, putting a duvet into a duvet cover isn't that complex a task, but when I left home, I knew of only one way to do it. I would feed the duvet into the duvet cover, like pushing a pen into a pen lid and then spend ages trying to get the corners of the duvet to fit into the corners of the cover. I often ended up inside the cover, with the duvet, trying to push the corners into the right spot to make the duvet fit smoothly.

Then a friend showed me an easier way. If I turned the cover inside out, put my hands inside the cover and up to the top corners, then I could grab the corresponding corners of the duvet and simply unroll the cover down over the duvet. Something that previously took me 20 minutes now took me 2, and the result was much better.

Obviously, academic learning is much more complex than putting a cover on a duvet but, that said, there are some similarities. I persisted with my old way of putting the duvet on because I didn't realise there was a more effective method. Paying attention to what we are doing and learning the most effective methods and strategies can improve our effectiveness and efficiency.

Adopting effective methods can improve your learning; as you notice this, you can increase your sense of mastery, feel more confident, be less anxious and enjoy your studies more.

Making memories

In the previous chapter, we discussed the fact that when you are asleep your brain clears out information that you don't need and moves important learning to your long-term memory.

To do this, your brain has to decide what memories are important and should be retained and what memories can be stripped away. There are a number of elements that tell your brain that something you have learned is important:

1   Repetition – if we do something over and over again, it clearly must have importance and value, and so it is more likely to be retained.

2   Effort expended – learning that makes us work hard leaves a deep imprint. In effect, this means that to learn effectively, we need to put in some significant effort. If it is too easy, we are likely to forget it.

3   Emotional association – if something makes us excited, passionate, scared or upset, we are much more likely to remember it than something that has no emotional content for us.

4   Connections – making connections between knowledge already securely stored in your memory and new learning can give the new learning something to stick to, meaning that you're more likely to hold onto it.

5 Narrative – we are story-telling animals who are programmed to find and remember patterns. Using new learning to add to old stories or create new stories will make it easier to remember. For example, remembering a reference for a journal article (name and date) is much easier if you can fit it into a larger narrative that explains how something works or how something occurred. Trying to remember the reference alone is likely to be much more difficult.

Taking control of your learning

In my experience, most students spend a lot of time working to increase their subject knowledge and focussing on doing well on specific pieces of work without ever really considering how they can improve their learning skills. They try to improve their performance by working harder and longer but not necessarily by being more effective. Taking some time out to think about how you can learn best can deliver exponential improvements.

There are three elements to think about when considering how to improve your learning [6]:

- understanding yourself as a learner – knowing how you learn best and what factors can help or hinder your learning. For example, do you learn best by yourself or when working with others?
- understanding a range of effective learning strategies and techniques
- knowing which strategy or technique to use in different circumstances or for different types of learning

To take control, you need to avoid simply repeating the same routine and instead monitor your learning, experiment with different strategies and routines, and evaluate how effective they are for you. We're going to look at some techniques below that evidence suggests are effective (and a few that aren't), but you can find more examples in the references and online. Remember, nothing works for everyone but everyone can find something that works for them. Keep experimenting and trying new strategies, and you will grow as a learner and become a stronger and more confident student.

Beware the zombie myth of learning styles

I mentioned above that it is helpful for you to know how you personally learn best. However, what I don't mean by that is that you should identify your 'learning style'.

Learning styles were very popular a few years ago – students were identified as being audio, visual or kinaesthetic learners, and teachers and lecturers were supposed to adopt their teaching to meet each student's learning style.

Unfortunately, the evidence suggests that the idea of learning styles is essentially nonsense [7].

A wealth of evidence now indicates that learning styles don't meet tests of scientific validity and that they aren't reliable categories. (You may appear to be one type of learner today and another next month.) More concerning still, if you try to learn only in your 'preferred style', you will actually learn less [8].

Ignore the idea of learning styles and focus instead on practical aspects that you find helpful and strategies that are actually supported by solid evidence.

Don't be put off by what you don't yet know or understand

When I started my psychotherapy training, I was making a leap from a completely different discipline. I had always been an arts-and-humanities student (my first degree is in drama) but was now moving to a different faculty and different language and different ways of looking at the world. On my first day in class, I had a moment of panic. The people around me were speaking words that I didn't understand and talking comfortably about concepts that I'd never encountered. My immediate thoughts were 'What am I doing here? I don't belong. I don't understand anything. I don't think I can do this'.

This was a very mild episode of something called imposter syndrome and is actually very common. Not knowing or understanding something can make us feel vulnerable, especially if we believe that our lack of knowledge might be exposed to others (by being asked a question in class or a test, for instance). We worry about being judged or humiliated, and that worry triggers an emotional hijack, which in turn makes it more difficult to acquire the knowledge we currently don't have.

In fact, not knowing something or not being able to understand it yet is a vital part of the process of learning. The entire field of scientific discovery is based on the phrase 'we don't know'. When we identify that we don't know something, we can take action to find that knowledge. By acknowledging what you don't know or understand, you are creating the conditions for learning to take place. After all, the whole point of being at university is to learn things you don't already know. If you knew everything already, there would be little point in spending years studying the subject.

Being aware of what you don't know or don't understand means that you are working. If you are willing to embrace doubt and keep working, you will eventually acquire the knowledge and understanding that you seek.

At university level, you will probably encounter concepts and ideas that are difficult to understand at first and you may have to explore these ideas several times and in different ways before you get them. This is perfectly normal and is actually a well-studied phenomenon in education. We call these ideas 'threshold concepts' [9] – you step through a threshold into a new way of understanding, interpreting or thinking about something. The moment of stepping through the threshold is a 'eureka' moment, when everything becomes clearer, but before that comes a period of not understanding. The fact that we have a label for this experience shows that it is a common phenomenon.

So, if you don't understand something, don't panic. It doesn't mean you aren't good enough or that you don't belong at university. It just means that you are at a particular point in your learning journey. Try to break down what you don't understand into smaller chunks. Work methodically through it, piece by piece, to build your understanding over time and use the support available to help you with whatever you find most difficult. This could be your tutor, a study skills advisor or a peer on your course, or you may find some helpful explanations online or in related books in your library.

Remember, doubt is your friend. It is helping by guiding you to what you don't know, so you can fill in the gaps in your knowledge and build your understanding. Question the doubt, so it can help you more, by asking it specific questions – 'What is it I don't understand?' 'Are there parts of this that do make sense?' 'What might the barriers be to my understanding this?' 'Do I understand the words and terms being used – if not, would it help to work on this before trying to understand the larger concept?' and so on.

Effective learning strategies

So what learning techniques are effective and which aren't? For space reasons, I'm going to briefly explore a number of strategies below. If you are interested in reading about effective learning in more depth, you can find some recommendations for further reading at the end of the book.

Learning in the classroom/lecture theatre

1 **Maintaining concentration**
   How can you maintain 100% concentration on everything your lecturer says for the entire duration of a lecture or class? The answer is simple – you can't. That isn't to say that you can't learn effectively in a lecture or increase your ability to concentrate with practice – you can do both. But it is important to start from reality. The human brain naturally moves in and out of states of focussed attention – this actually aids your learning. If your lecturer says something that makes you think of something related or you start to wonder how it fits with something else, this will help to embed what you've just heard into your long-term memory. But you will miss the next thing your lecturer says.

   If you worry about naturally drifting out of concentration like this, you can end up in an anxiety spiral; you might think – 'I've missed what she just said, now I won't know everything, that means I won't understand this'. As a result, your emotions hijack you and you miss even more of the lecture.

Accept that your concentration is limited and simply refocus when you become aware that you've moved into an unfocussed state.

You can also aid concentration by asking yourself questions about what you are hearing and taking part in classroom discussions. Some people also find that doodling can help them to concentrate for longer.

2　Reducing distractions
Switch off your phone. There is now a significant body of evidence that demonstrates that having your phone switched on, even if you don't look at it, will reduce your learning [10]. This is partly because your brain will continue to monitor the phone for notifications [11].

Some research also suggests that having a laptop in class can reduce your learning [12]. Screens naturally draw our attention. If you do need a laptop in class (e.g., if you have dysgraphia and need a laptop for note-taking), try to disable or remove all social media and switch off access to the internet until the lecture is over [13].

3　Taking effective notes
There are two reasons for taking notes. The first is to act as a record of the lecture so you can use the notes to study with later. The second is to improve your learning while in the lecture or class. Research has clearly shown that taking notes improves learning [14].

However, what generally isn't helpful is to try to take verbatim notes of everything your lecturer says. Remember, this lecture isn't the only time you can access this information; your lecturer will have drawn from the research literature to put the lecture together. You can read the same literature. Let go of trying to take verbatim notes and instead focus on taking notes that might be useful.

Increasingly, you may also find that the lecture will be recorded for you to revisit later and your lecturer may provide some notes as a starting point for you.

Taking notes is actually a complicated cognitive process. You need to take in what your lecturer is saying, extract key information and ideas, connect this with previous learning, paraphrase or summarise all of this and then write down some notes. This is a good thing – remember what we said earlier about the fact that we need to make some effort to build memories.

It's another reason why writing verbatim notes is less helpful – if you just try to copy down what is being said, you aren't thinking about it, and so it can all slip out of your memory.

There are models of note-taking that you can research and try for yourself. However, to maximise your note-taking, it can be helpful to begin by focussing on listening and noting down the major points, questions you may still have, anything you haven't yet understood and links to your previous learning. Some students also find it helpful to draw some of their notes using diagrams or pictures [15].

4 **Making your notes more effective later**
Research has also shown that if you rewrite your notes after class, they become more helpful as revision aids and that the act of rewriting improves your retention of what you learned in class.

Studying by yourself

1 **Spacing**
One of the most effective ways of imprinting new learning on your memory and ensuring that you can recall it when needed is to study it repeatedly with increasing gaps in between [16]. By allowing yourself to begin forgetting the material and then refreshing it, you will not only ensure that it is firmly held in your memory but also find it easier to recall [17].

For instance, let's suppose you have a lecture on a new subject on Monday. On Tuesday, you could revisit your notes and rewrite them (as suggested above). You could revisit the subject on Friday (three days later), testing to see how much you remember and understand. Return to the subject the following Friday and then again in 2 weeks' time. Research has shown that this method significantly improves learning and you will be able to recall what you have learned, for a much longer period of time, than if you just tried to study the subject in one go.

2 Retrieval practice
Why do we ask students to complete tests or exams? The most obvious answer is that it allows us to assess how well you have learned something, but testing has a more important effect. Testing improves memory retention and memory recall [18]. Taking a test in a subject improves your knowledge and understanding of that subject. This is something we've known for many years but only recently have educators begun to discuss it as a study strategy for students [19].

As we discussed in the section above, one of the key elements to storing something securely in your memory is to make your brain work hard on it. (Some researchers call this 'desirable difficulty'.) Testing yourself is a harder task than simply re-reading, and that extra effort helps you remember it better. Added to this, when we recall something, we actually recode it in our brains, meaning it is more securely stored.

This means that testing is actually a form of retrieval practice – you are practising remembering what you have learned and practising in this way improves your learning. As an added benefit, it also helps you to identify gaps in your knowledge so you can more effectively target and learn things that you don't know. Over time, tests can also provide you with objective evidence that your knowledge is increasing and so boost your confidence and self-esteem. Make self-testing a part of your study routine.

3 Explain the why and the how of what you know.
Studying for understanding is often more effective than just trying to remember facts – when we understand something, the facts tend to stick to our understanding, making them easier to recall.

One way of doing this is to explain what you are learning [20]. Imagine teaching the material to an inquisitive person who knows nothing about your subject but who, like a toddler, is going to keep asking 'why?' Why does it do that? Why does that happen? See if you can explain it to that person and answer all of their questions.

It can also help to ask how what you have learned links up with other material you have already covered. Finding explanations for this will also deepen your understanding.

4 **Reflective practice**
To take control of your learning, it can help if you pay attention to how well and how much you are learning. To do this, we have to engage in what we call 'reflective practice'. This simply means spending some time deliberately and consciously thinking about your learning experience so you can learn better in the future.

Thinking about your learning progress, in this way, has a number of benefits. It can help you to identify how far you've come and so build your confidence that you are learning. It can help you to identify skills or knowledge that you want to strengthen in the future. It can also help to increase your understanding of what you have learned and, by doing so, embed your learning more securely in your memory.

You may want to pay attention to two aspects: what you are learning and how you are learning. There are a few exercises that may help with this:

What you have learned

- Think about something you have learned and consider it from multiple perspectives – what do you think about it? What would family members think about it? What does your lecturer think about it? What would a newspaper say about it? What does the research literature say about it?

- At the end of a class, write down three or four things that you have learned that you did not know or fully understand before.

How you have learned

- Take one of the topics you are studying this semester. Try to think back to before you started this class and identify what you knew before you started. Then identify what you know now (how much you have learned). Then think about what you want to learn next – what are the gaps in your knowledge you want to fill? What are you curious about?

- After a class, you may want to think about one aspect of what you have learned. (It may help to use a different aspect each time.) For instance, what did you learn today that you found most interesting? What did you learn that was exciting? What did you learn that was most difficult to understand? Then think about why you found it interesting, exciting or difficult. This may identify some areas of further study that you would like to explore or know more about.

The best aid to reflective practice is often the feedback that you receive from lecturers or tutors, whether in class or on an assignment. Pay attention to any feedback you receive and think about how you can use it to improve your learning in the future.

5 **Be flexible about your study routine.**
Students sometimes get rigid in their thinking and allow themselves to study only in 'perfect' conditions. They might think, 'There's no point in studying now, I only have 1 hour and I need 3 hours for it to be worth it' or 'My study space is in my bedroom, I can't possibly study effectively anywhere else'.

These thoughts are good examples of anxiety manipulating us to avoid doing something that would help us be more in control and feel better. In fact, studying in short bursts and in different places can help us remember and recall what we have learned [16]. When paired with the spacing technique described above, short intensive bursts of study can actually be more effective than studying a subject for one long 3-hour block.

Studying in different places also helps us to improve recall – this is partly due to the way in which our brain associates what we've learned with the environment we were in when we learned it. If you study only in your bedroom, it will be easier to recall what you've learned in your bedroom than in an exam room. If you study in three or four places, it will be easier to recall what you've learned when you are in a fifth place.

We'll look at some more specific learning techniques for particular types of assessment in later chapters.

Ineffective learning strategies

Unfortunately, two of the most common learning strategies that students employ appear to be far less effective – these are re-reading and highlighting notes [16, 18, 20]. That's not to say that you can't learn from reading generally. It's just that re-reading material that we already sort of know doesn't demand enough from our brain, and so no learning takes place – the same is true of highlighting. Remember, to learn, make your brain do some work.

Don't forget the basics!

Employing effective learning strategies will definitely help, but don't forget that you and your brain are biological things. Remember, when you are studying, to stay hydrated, rest, top up your energy levels with healthy food and take breaks in the sunlight if possible. All of this will also improve your learning and your wellbeing.

Why those dull subjects might be important

Remember those three dull subjects I asked you to think about earlier? These are some of the reasons they can actually be important and interesting, as suggested by students:

● The brightness of street lights

Some students argued that bright street lights have a negative impact on the environment, causing light pollution and in some cases interrupting the cyclical rhythms of nocturnal animals, which get confused about whether it is day or night. Others pointed out that street lights have been shown to reduce crime, particularly violent crime against women – this has led to one or two vigorous debates in class.

● The history of socks

Socks actually have a long history, but one student suggested that you could use a study of socks as a way of looking at class and industrialisation. Fine silk socks were once a status symbol for the nobility, while working people produced their own rough-spun versions simply to keep warm. The invention of the knitting machine and then the introduction of nylon led to a democratisation of the sock as wealth inequality decreased in the twentieth century. However, some might argue that the appearance of expensive designer socks provides an example of the growth of inequality in the early twenty-first century.

● Finance and accounting in contemporary theatre

A number of students suggested that the arts play a vital role in shaping culture and contemporary beliefs. However, a heavily marketised theatre sector promotes one type of view and production, squeezing out diverse voices and important experimental work. By understanding how finance and accounting work, we can ensure that more voices are represented in theatre and prevent a monoculture from developing.

Further reading

How we learn

Carey, B. (2015). *How We Learn.* London: Pan Books.

De Bruyckere, P., Kirchner, P. A. & Hulshof, C. D. (2015). *Urban Myths About Learning and Education.* Oxford: Elsevier Academic Press.

Hattie, J. & Yates, G. (2014). *Visible Learning and the Science of How We Learn.* London: Routledge.

Effective studying

Brick, J., Wilson, N., Wong, D. & Herke, M. (2018). *Academic Success: A Student's Guide to Studying at University.* London: Red Globe Press.

Cottrell, S. (2019). *The Study Skills Handbook* (5th ed). London: Red Globe Press.

References

1 Haggis, T. (2003). Constructing Images of Ourselves? A Critical Investigation into 'Approaches to Learning' Research in Higher Education. *British Educational Research Journal*, 29(1), 89–104.

2 Trigwell, K. & Prosser, M. (1991). Improving the Quality of Student Learning: The Influence of Learning Context and Student Approaches to Learning on Learning Outcomes. *Higher Education*, 22(3), 251–266.

3 Postareff, L., Mattsson, M., Lindblom-Ylänne, S. & Hailikari, T. (2016). The Complex Relationship Between Emotions, Approaches to Learning, Study Success and Study Progress During the Transition to University. *Higher Education*, 73(3), 441–457. doi:https://doi.org/10.1007/s10734-016-0096-7.

4 Asikainen, H., Salmela-Aro, K., Parpala, A. & Katajavuori, N. (2019). Learning Profiles and Their Relation to Study-Related Burnout and Academic Achievement Among University Students. *Learning and Individual Differences*. doi:https://doi.org/10.1016/j.lindif.2019.101781.

5 Goldacre, B. (2009). *Bad Science.* London: Harper Perennial.

6 Schraw, G., Crippen, K. J. & Hartley, K. (2006). Promoting Self-Regulation in Science Education: Metacognition as Part of a Broader Perspective on Learning. *Research in Science Education*, 36, 111–139.

7 Kirschner, P. (2017). Stop Propagating the Learning Styles Myth. *Computers and Education*,106, 166–171.

8 De Bruyckere, P., Kirchner, P. A. & Hulshof, C. D. (2015). *Urban Myths About Learning and Education.* Oxford: Elsevier Academic Press.

9 Meyer, J. H. F. & Land, R. (2003). Threshold Concepts and Troublesome Knowledge: Linkages to Ways of Thinking and Practising. In: Rust, C. (Ed.), *Improving Student Learning – Ten Years On.* Oxford: OCSLD.

10 Felisoni, D. D. & Strommer Godoi, A. (2018). Cell Phone Usage and Academic Performance: An Experiment. *Computers and Education*, 117, 175–187.

11 Ward, A. F., Duke, K., Gneesy, A. & Bos, M. W. (2017). Brain Drain: The Mere Presence of One's Own Smartphone Reduces Available Cognitive Capacity. *Journal of the Association for Consumer Research*, 2(2), 140–154

12 Sana, F., Weston, T. & Cepeda, N. J. (2013). Laptop Multitasking Hinders Classroom Learning for Both Users and Nearby Peers. *Computers & Education*, 62, 24–31.

13 Ravizza, S. M., Uitvlugt, M. G. & Fenn, K. M. (2017). Logged in and Zoned Out: How Laptop Internet Use Relates to Classroom Learning. *Psychological Science*, 28, 1–10.

14 Kiewra, K. A. (2002). How Classroom Teachers Can Help Students Learn and Teach Them How to Learn. *Theory into Practice*, 41(2), 71–80.

15 Wammes, J. D., Meade, M. E. & Fernandes, M. A. (2016). The Drawing Effect: Evidence for Reliable and Robust Memory Benefits in Free Recall. *The Quarterly Journal of Experimental. Psychology*, 69(9):1752–1776.

16 Carey, B. (2015). *How We Learn.* London: Pan Books.

17 Dunlosky, J., Rawson, K. A., Marsh, E. J., Nathan, M. J. & Willingham, D. T. (2013). Improving Students Learning with Effective Learning Techniques: Promising Directions from Cognitive and Educational Psychology. *Psychological Science in the Public Interest*, 14, 4–58.

18 Roediger III, H. & Karpicke, J. D. (2006). The Power of Testing: Basic Research and Implications for Educational Practice. *Perspectives on Psychological Science*, 1(3), 181–120.

19 Spitzer, H. F. (1939). Studies in Retention. *The Journal of Educational Psychology*, 30(9), 641–656.

20 Roediger, H. L. & Pyc, M. A. (2012). Inexpensive Techniques to Improve Education: Applying Cognitive Psychology to Enhance Educational Practice. *Journal of Applied Research in Memory and Cognition*, 1(4), 242–248.

5 Socialising, belonging and learning

So far, we have identified that taking care of your wellbeing can improve your learning and that how you engage with your learning can affect your wellbeing. Now we need to take this one step further because not only are there links between wellbeing and learning but both are also affected by our relationships with the people around us.

As we saw from the models of wellbeing in Chapter 2, human beings are not solitary creatures. Our health and wellbeing benefit if we spend time focussing outside of ourselves and connecting with others. This isn't just about having other people there to support us when we need them (although that is important); it's also about the benefits we derive from supporting others, feeling part of a community and having fun. We are social animals, and our brain needs social interactions to function at its best.

Research in the field of social neuroscience demonstrates that being socially connected to other people has positive impacts, not only on our mood but also on our physical health and our cognitive functioning (i.e., on our ability to think). It may be surprising but social connection (or lack of it) can have some pretty direct and significant impacts on us and feeling lonely can change the way our bodies function at a cellular and genetic level.

Research has found the following:

- People who are socially well connected are 50% less likely to die prematurely [1]. Some investigators have theorised that the reason women live longer than men is that women have better social networks.

- Loneliness increases the likelihood that you will get a cold [2].
- Social ties appear to make it easier and more likely that you will adopt and maintain healthy lifestyle habits (like exercising, eating well and avoiding substance misuse) [3, 4].
- Loneliness appears to reduce the quality and efficiency of our sleep [5].
- Loneliness is linked with depression and with greater difficulty in managing stress [6].

What this means is that our social networks have a real and measurable impact on our physical and mental health. This doesn't mean that you need fear short periods of time on your own or transitions between old social networks and new environments. Loneliness, like all negative emotions, actually has a positive purpose – it is encouraging you to take action to address a current problem (to meet your needs in balance). Loneliness is an alarm that indicates that you should take some steps to increase your social connectedness. It is only when loneliness persists for a prolonged period of time that it can have negative effects.

Social wellbeing and learning

Not only does our social life impact on our wellbeing but it can also have some direct impacts on our ability to learn and perform to our academic ability. Researchers have found that being socially isolated can reduce our ability to focus our attention, concentrate, remember and problem-solve [7–9], and some research has even shown a direct impact on overall academic performance and grades [8, 10].

On the other side of the coin, we have long known that feeling a sense of social belonging within your university makes it more likely that you won't drop out and will perform well [11].

Of course, this doesn't mean that you should spend all of your time socialising to ward off the risk that occasionally feeling lonely will reduce your grades. Remember, this is about balance – although being socially isolated for a prolonged period of time may be a problem, doing nothing but socialising and partying will also reduce your learning, wellbeing and performance. We need time with others and time alone to consolidate our own thoughts and learning.

Learning can also be a profoundly social activity. Collaborating with others in class, engaging in debates, talking about your subject with peers and studying with others can help to build up your knowledge and understanding. All of this means that our learning and wellbeing can benefit from being part of a community of learners. Even if you are an online student or someone who because of other responsibilities can't be on campus outside of class time, you may benefit from using the opportunities you do have to build social connections in the classroom or online.

Finding and making friends at university

Let's start by asking this question first – What do we mean by friends?

I know the answer to that question might seem obvious, but it's worth thinking about. I've met many students who have thousands of 'friends' online but feel they have no genuine friends in the real world. Is a friend just someone you know and like? How long do you have to know somebody before you can call them a friend? How many close friends is it possible to have?

This can get particularly tricky if you're having a bad time in your life – if you feel you have no one you can talk to, does that mean that all of those people you know aren't 'real friends'?

If you're someone who finds social life easy, all of these questions may seem unnecessary to you. But time and time again, I've worked with students who find this subject difficult and worry that, somehow, they aren't doing it right or that their friends aren't real friends because they don't meet some specific definition or template in the student's head. So it's worth taking a moment to think about this and to acknowledge that there isn't a right way to do this and there is no one fixed way that someone can be your friend.

The truth is that we need many different types of people in our lives. A friend with whom you have fun, but wouldn't talk to about your personal problems, is still a friend. The fact that they are someone you can have fun with means they are fulfilling an important role in your life and helping you meet an underlying need.

Of course, we also need friends we can be close to and turn to for comfort or support when we need it – but, in general, we should expect to have fewer of these types of friends, as getting to that point in a relationship takes longer.

Aristotle suggested that we should think about three types of friendship: friends of convenience, friends based on shared interests or pleasures and friends of emotional intimacy [12, 13].

Friends of convenience are the most common types of friendships. These are friendships that are primarily useful to you both – you are helpful to each other, and this is what maintains the relationship.

This may be a flatmate, for instance; you might pool your food money to make it go further or take turns cooking for each other, and this makes your flat a nicer place to be. Or it may be a course mate, and you help each other to understand the most difficult parts of your degree, and if one of you is absent, the other picks up extra handouts and relays important information. Or it may be someone with whom you share lifts or child care.

These friendships are not to be undervalued as they make life easier for both of you – they are the kinds of friendships that often oil the wheels of life. Having a number of them can make your day-to-day experience easier. But it's also important not to expect too much from them. When the friendship stops being useful (you move out of the same flat, leave university, or your children grow up and apart), it isn't unusual for the relationship to come to an end completely. This doesn't mean there is anything fundamentally wrong with either of you as a person. It's just how these friendships work; the cement that holds them together is that they meet a need for both of you, and once that is no longer the case you separate.

Sometimes, a friendship that starts out of convenience can develop over time to become much more significant. We'll look at how this can happen in the next section.

Friendships based on shared interests or pleasures are the next most common types of friendship. These might be friends that you meet in a student union society or club, for example – you might both enjoy the same sport, campaign for the same political movement or you might just make each other laugh.

These shared interests and pleasures mean that these relationships can be closer than friendships of convenience. You may naturally find that you have more in common, and this means you will find each other's company pleasant and enjoyable.

However, if one of you loses interest in the thing that originally brought you together, these friendships can also come to an end. You can sometimes find this with old friends who you haven't seen for a while. Once upon a time, you may have found it easy to find things to talk about, but now that you have very different lives and interests, conversation dries up quickly, once you're done talking about old times. Again, this is completely normal.

Friendships based on shared pleasures are a vital part of our social network, as they help us to meet our needs and to discover more about ourselves and what we like. They can also be a source of fun – which is important in and of itself. More important still is that, over time, friendships like these can lead to the third type of friendship.

Friendships of emotional intimacy are the closest and also the rarest types of friendship. These relationships will tend to endure much longer because they are based on how much the two friends care for each other and a shared sense of good will and love. As a result, these friendships can outlast changes in lifestyle, interest and circumstance.

Building a relationship like this tends to take time. There are good reasons for this – close friendships require a great deal of trust, and it makes sense not to extend too much trust to people you've just met. Rather, it is often better to gradually extend trust as you get to know someone better.

Because building these friendships takes time, you should expect to have fewer of them. Finding someone suited to being a close friend can also be more difficult – which is why it's important to create multiple opportunities for you to meet the right people. If you assume you'll meet your best friend ever in your flat or on your course, you're placing all of your eggs in one basket and may end up disappointed.

Instead, it can be more helpful to seek out and create lots of opportunities. Remember, universities tend to be big places with thousands of students in them; there is every chance that someone in that university could be a close friend to you – but you have to give yourself the chance to meet them.

Taking a structured approach to finding and making friends

Thinking about friendship in this way means that you can build a clear plan to help you find new friends – whether you've just started university or you've been there a while and feel you need more friends in your life.

Rather than trying to identify the one place where you might find a close friend you can be emotionally intimate with, focus on opportunities to find friendships of convenience and friendships based on shared interests or pleasures. You need these friendships anyway, and the more of these relationships you have, the more chance there is that one of them will develop into a close friendship.

You might want to build an action plan or mind map of possible opportunities that you can target. It might help to make a list of the things you are interested in now or have enjoyed in the past. Then you can look for groups or activities that are happening in your university that match up to your interests. Many universities hold induction or orientation weeks at the beginning of university, during which events are organised to help you find and join societies or activities. You can usually also find information on your university's website.

Sometimes, students tell me that they don't really have any interests or hobbies and therefore don't know what societies to join. This is easily explainable. As we grow and mature, our interests often change, so you may have fallen out of love with previous hobbies. Many students have also devoted a lot of their time to studying and passing exams so they could get to university and therefore may have abandoned old interests. That means that this is an opportunity to discover new interests and hobbies. One of the great things about being a student is that you get to try out new things – so if you don't know what to try, pick a few things at random and give them a go. It may also make sense to look for friendships in the places you'll already be – class, student accommodation, study skills groups, and so on.

Once you've mapped this out, chose two or three of these opportunities to target first. This may simply be asking a classmate for a coffee after class or it could be contacting a society online to arrange to attend their next event or meeting. If it helps, you can use social media to make the first connections and to set up meetings in real life.

Accept from the beginning that not all of your efforts will result in your finding friends. You may go to a social gathering and realise you don't want to spend time with the people there again. If that is genuinely the case, it is fine. Remember, you aren't expecting to find the perfect social group straight away. This is why it's important to try out a number of opportunities.

However, do take some time to review that decision and make sure it is the right decision for you. Sometimes, anxiety or loneliness can make us reject social connections that could actually turn out to be good for us. We can become more critical and easily dissatisfied that people don't perfectly match what we need. Stop and ask yourself – even if the person or people you met aren't perfect, could they still be friends of convenience or friends of shared interest? Could they plug a small hole in your social life, even if they aren't the entire answer?

If the answer is definitely no, then you've ruled something out and can move on to the next set of opportunities.

Creating a plan like this can help you to develop concrete actions and a structured way of building a new social network. Thinking about improving your social life can often feel vague and foggy. It may be something you want to do but without any clear sense of how to move forward. Having a plan can take away this lack of clarity and give you a solid structure to guide your actions.

But what if I'm shy or socially anxious?

First of all, let's be clear, it is ok to be shy. Most social groups need a combination of outgoing people, shy people and people in between. If you want to sit on the edge of a group, enjoying the conversation and only occasionally joining in, that's fine. What you have to say, when you do speak, will probably be worth saying.

All groups also need people who are good at listening. If you're more comfortable in this role, then you can help the groups you're in by being a person who listens more than talks. You can play an active role in conversations simply by asking people about themselves, their experiences and how they feel. In time, as you become more comfortable with people, you may feel more able to add in some of your own experiences and thoughts.

Accepting and embracing your shyness as a potential positive will make it easier for you to find groups of friends that suit you and to enjoy social gatherings. Usually, the problem with being shy isn't that you may be quiet, it's that you think you 'shouldn't' be quiet or that you 'should' say more. Embrace who you are in groups, and people will adapt to that and be attracted to you.

On the other hand, social anxiety – which prevents you from engaging socially or causes you great distress – is not ok. Nor does it have to be with you forever. We discussed anxiety in more detail in **Chapter 3.** If you experience social anxiety, you will probably find it useful to read that section, but here are some specific tips on overcoming social anxiety:

1 Accept that having nervous feelings before meeting new people is normal and ok. Actually, even if you've met people before, it isn't unusual to experience a few nerves before a social occasion. If you accept these feelings, flow with them but still go ahead and meet people, they will dissipate natu-rally. It's often only when we fight the feeling and try to force it away or start to think 'Oh no, I'm anxious' that normal nerves become really unpleasant anxiety.

2 Be aware of a social anxiety thought loop, which goes like this – 'I'm too anxious to meet people in case they don't like me, because then I'll be ostracised and have no friends, so I will stay in my bedroom and not meet people, which will result in me having no friends'. This loop results in our making sure that the thing we fear comes true. Alternatively, what you might fear is the pain of rejection. Anxiety can make you believe that staying in your room is safer than risking the

feeling that comes from people not liking you. Remember that being isolated doesn't keep you safe – it has real effects on your physical and emotional health, and spending time with people who are genuinely friends isn't dangerous. Finding friends is possible and when you find them they will be beneficial for your wellbeing – there are people out there who will like you. Don't let anxiety stop you from finding them.

3 Experiment to see how your social anxiety behaves – so you can tame it. Some people find it helpful to test out the ideas that social anxiety generates. For instance, you might deliberately say something silly to see whether the result really is that no one ever speaks to you again. Or you might want to start dancing for no reason, just to show that you can and that anxiety isn't in control. When you do this, anxiety loses its power.

4 Rehearse positive scenarios in advance – anxiety will try to get you to imagine all the ways a social event might go wrong. Don't argue with that; instead, add some more positive scenarios and some scenarios that are just ok. They don't have to be realistic, they will still dilute the power of anxiety's negative imagination.

5 After a social event, anxiety might want you to think about all of the moments in the evening that weren't perfect, dissecting them and imagining all the negative thoughts people must have had about you. Accept that every social event will have a moment in it that wasn't perfect, but add to these thoughts those moments that you did enjoy, when things did go well or when you helped someone else.

6 Don't be afraid to use support – if there is a counselling service in your university, you may find that accessing some sessions can help you develop more strategies to overcome social anxiety.

Classroom discussion and participation

Research shows that students who actively participate in classroom discussions and activities learn more and perform better [14, 15]. Taking an active role in discussions helps you to learn more deeply, improves your understanding of the subject and increases your ability to remember the content of the class [16, 17]. Discussion can also help you to check what you have learnt and correct any errors in your understanding.

Classroom discussions are also a chance to engage socially with your peers in a way that is structured and safe. You don't have to think of something to talk about or what you should ask next to keep the conversation going – all of that is already laid out for you. However, within the conversation, you can start to make connections with your peers – you may, for instance, discover that you share common interests or passions in an aspect of your subject or common things you don't like or understand. These connections can give you the starting point for conversations that can continue outside class.

Of course, some classroom discussions are easier to participate in than others. Most students find it easier to engage in small group discussions, where the lecturer isn't listening in [14]. These discussions also offer you the greatest chance to participate and make connections with your peers.

Joining in discussions can be more difficult if you're in a lecture theatre with a large number of students. Because of the layout and format of a lecture, these discussions can often be confined to the lecturer's asking and answering questions and facilitating debate in front of the whole class. It isn't unusual to feel nervous about speaking in these circumstances – whether or not you consider yourself to be shy in other situations. Nevertheless, if you can join in by asking questions, volunteering to answer your lecturer's questions or by giving your opinion, you can improve your own learning and that of your classmates. Let's look at some ways you can overcome any nerves that might get in the way.

Accept your nerves as a normal response to the environment

Research shows that most students feel anxious about speaking in lectures and large classes [18]. Feeling a little nervous is perfectly normal. Accept this and don't let the feeling mislead you. Sometimes, students interpret the presence of nervousness as a sign that they aren't good enough or that it is evidence that they aren't confident or clever enough to speak. This isn't the case. Even lecturers get nervous at the start of a class. Take a moment to accept the feeling as being normal and ok, breathe, use one of the relaxation techniques in this book (e.g., 7/11 breathing on page 23), clarify in your head what you want to say and then join in.

Be prepared

You will find it easier to join in if you feel you already have a little understanding of the subject under discussion [14, 19]. If your question is from an informed perspective, you will feel more confident in asking it. You can increase your preparedness by doing any pre-class reading, looking at any notes or slides your lecturer has provided in advance and spending a little time familiarising yourself with the key terms online.

Feel the gratitude of your classmates

Remember, because most students feel nervous about speaking in lectures [18], if you ask or answer a question, you take the pressure off the other students in your class. You will also be helping to improve their learning.

Find your passion

It's easier to push nerves, about speaking, to one side when you are positively motivated to know more [20]. If there is a specific element of the class that you are more interested in or passionate about, make that the focus of your contribution.

Whatever you say, you won't be the only one thinking it

If you haven't understood something, then there will be others in your class who feel the same way. Your question will help them and you.

Don't feel that what you say has to be grammatically perfect or eloquent

When we're grappling with new ideas or concepts, we can often struggle to find the right way to express ourselves. This is ok. It shows you are learning new things and are genuinely engaged. Don't worry about sounding perfect; just focus on communicating the meaning of what you want to ask or say.

Keeping discussions going outside of class

Classroom discussions can be a way to start building a community that can support your learning and wellbeing. You can continue to build this community outside the classroom. This might be in an informal way, such as going for a coffee after class with some of your classmates or simply keeping the class discussion going on the bus.

Alternatively, you might be able to set up or use more formal forums. Many courses now have online discussion forums or social media groups – if yours doesn't have one, perhaps you could set one up. Your university may also have a student society for your subject, or you and some of your peers may like to set up a study group to support each other's learning.

Forums like this can help you to feel more connected, build your social network and improve your learning.

Feeling lonely

Loneliness can be a horrible feeling. However, as we discussed above, loneliness can be a useful warning sign – to encourage you to become more socially connected. This doesn't necessarily mean spending lots more time with other people. (It is possible to be surrounded by others but still feel lonely.) Rather, it may be the balance of how you spend your time that needs your attention.

Loneliness dissipates when we feel a genuine connection with others. One of the most effective ways of reducing loneliness is to look for opportunities to help other people [10]. When we help and support other people, we focus outside of ourselves and connect with another person's needs in a meaningful way. This helps us in a number of ways – we feel useful, we feel like a more active part of our community and we feel more connected to the person we are helping.

This is the case when we support one person, but we can get similar benefits from volunteering or working for causes bigger than ourselves – many universities offer volunteering opportunities or chances to join campaigns for causes like social justice or the environment.

Of course, the feeling of loneliness can make you feel that you are unable to help anyone else. Loneliness can make us focus in on ourselves and convince us that we have nothing to offer. It can also make you hypervigilant when you are in social situations, looking out only for signs that things are going wrong and ignoring things that go well or that you enjoy.

Be aware that these feelings are normal but they are not telling you the truth. Try not to argue with the thoughts; instead, turn your attention to mapping out your current social interactions and building a plan, as we discussed above. You may want to begin by looking for small opportunities to help others – giving up a seat on the bus, for instance, then building step by step from there. You may also benefit from talking to a counsellor or advisor, who can help you to build and act on your plan.

Maintaining old networks

Although moving into the new environment of a university will tend to focus your attention on building new friendships, it can be helpful to maintain your old networks as well. Staying in regular contact with those who know you well can help you feel you have a firm foundation supporting you. Thankfully, keeping in contact with close friends and family is now much easier, even if you've moved to go to university, as a result of social media.

Of course, speaking over the phone or online isn't the same as actually being with the other person and it might not feel as good. Even if you are commuting to university from home, you may find that your new routine and their routine don't always align, which makes it more difficult to have impromptu chats, as you once would have done. When this happens, it can feel like the relationship is drifting away or that the other person doesn't care about keeping in touch – which is probably not what is happening.

Maintaining old networks once you become a student can require some time, some care and some thought. Not only will your day-to-day timetable change but you yourself will probably go through some changes in taste, interest and outlook. This doesn't mean you can't keep your old friends. (Remember, friends of emotional intimacy can endure, even when interests change.) It just means you need to plan and think about how you do it.

It may help to set some regular times to catch up or to agree how often you will communicate, so you don't misread each other's behaviour. It can also help if you bear in mind that they aren't having your experience – make sure, in your conversations, that you focus as much on what is happening in their lives as you chat about what is happening in yours. If you're going to be busy, let them know in advance so they understand if you aren't in touch as often. Similarly, try to be accepting if things in their life mean they aren't available.

If things aren't working between you at any point, try to discuss it without apportioning blame or making each other feel guilty. Good relationships aren't defined by the absence of any conflict but by the fact that when conflict does arise, it is addressed without blame and resolved.

If your old relationships are helpful to you, then you can maintain them, even if you've moved a long way away.

Maintaining a social balance throughout the year

The academic year tends to have its own social rhythms. The beginning of the year tends to be busier, as people are getting to know one another or are catching up with old friends. Towards the end of the year, it isn't unusual for students to start withdrawing socially to focus on coursework and preparing for exams.

Although it is easy to see why these peaks and troughs in social activity exist, it is important to maintain a good social balance throughout the year. As we saw in **Chapter 2**, too much fun and too much time alone can both have an adverse effect. You may find that both your wellbeing and your academic performance benefit from pushing slightly against these peaks and troughs.

At the start of the year, it does make sense to spend time making new friendships or cementing old friendships after the long break. But don't let this distract you completely from your academic work. Spending 4 weeks partying and then trying to catch up can undermine your engagement, learning and performance. Remember, it is easier to establish and maintain good study habits at the beginning of the year (we cover this in **Chapter 6**)

Equally, at the end of the year, it makes sense to focus on your assessments and exams, but your performance will benefit from taking breaks and spending time with friends. Having some fun can reduce your stress levels, allowing you to concentrate and learn more effectively. Spending time with others can also help you retain a sense of perspective.

You don't stop being a human being just because you have exams coming up. Feed your brain the social contact it needs so you can perform to your potential.

Further reading

Importance of social connections

Cacioppo, J. T. & Patrick, W. (2008). *Loneliness.* New York: Norton.

Pinker, S. (2014). *The Village Effect: Why Face-to-Face Contact Matters.* London: Atlantic.

References

1   Holt-Lundstad, J., Smith, T. B. & Layton, J. B. (2010). Social Relationships and Mortality Risk: A Meta-Analytic Review. *PLoS Med*, 7(7), e1000316.

2   LeRoy, A. S. Murdock, K. W., Jaremka, L. M., Loya, A. & Faqundes, C. P. (2017). Loneliness Predicts Self-Reported Cold Symptoms After a Viral Challenge. *Health Psychology*, 36, 512–520.

3   Umberson, D., Crosnoe, R. & Reczek, C. (2010). Social Relationships and Health Behavior Across Life Course. *Annual Review Sociology*, 36, 139–157.

4   Kleiber, P., Whillans, A. V. & Chen, F. S. (2018). Long-Term Health Implications of Students' Friendship Formation During the Transition to University. *Applied Psychology: Health and Well-Being*, 10(2), 290–308. doi:https://doi.org/10.1111/aphw.12131.

5   Hayley, A. C., Downey, L. A., Stough, C., Sivertsen, B., Knapstad, M. & Øverland, S. (2017). Social and Emotional Loneliness and Self-Reported Difficulty Initiating and Maintaining Sleep (DIMS) in a Sample of Norwegian University Students. *Scandinavian Journal of Psychology*, 58(1), 91–99.

6   Mushtaq, R., Shoib, S., Shah, T. & Mushtaq, S. (2014). Relationship Between Loneliness, Psychiatric Disorders and Physical Health? A Review on the Psychological Aspects of Loneliness. *Journal of Clinical & Diagnostic Research*, 8(9), WE01–WE04.

7   Cacioppo, J. T., Ernst, J. M., Burleson, M. H., McClintock, M. K., Malarkey, W. B., Hawkley, L. C., Kowalewski, R. B., Paulsen, A., Hobson, J. A., Hugdahl, K., Spiegel, D. & Berntson, G. G. (2000). Lonely Traits and Concomitant Physiological Processes: The MacArthur Social Neuroscience Studies. *International Journal of Psychophysiology*, 35, 143–154.

8   Baumeister, R. F., Twenge, J. M. & Nuss, C. K. (2002). Effects of Social Exclusion on Cognitive Processes: Anticipated Aloneness Reduces Intelligent Thought. *Journal of Personality and Social Psychology*, 83(4), 817–827.

9   Jaremka, L. M., Peng, J., Bornstein, R., Alfano, C. M., Andridge, R. R., Povoski, S. P., Lipari, A. M., Agnese, D. M., Farrar, W. B., Yee, L. D., Carson, W. E. 3rd & Kiecolt-Glaser, J. K. (2014). Cognitive Problems Among Breast Cancer Survivors: Loneliness Enhances Risk. *Psycho-oncology*, 23(12), 1356-1364.

10 Cacioppo, J. T. & Patrick, W. (2008). *Loneliness.* New York: Norton.

11 Tinto, V. (1975). Dropout from Higher Education: A Theoretical Synthesis of Recent Research. *Review of Educational Research*, 45(1), 89–125.

12 Hall, E. (2018). *Aristotle's Way.* London: Bodley Head.

13 Aristotle. (2011). Aristotle's *Nicomachean Ethics*. R. C. Bartlett & S. D. Collins. (trans.). Chicago: Chicago University Press.

14 Rocca, K. A. (2010). Student Participation in the College Classroom: An Extended Multidisciplinary Literature Review. *Communication Education*, 59(2), 185–213, doi:https://doi.org/10.1080/03634520903505936.

15 Lyons, P. R. (1989). Assessing Classroom Participation. *College Teaching*, 37, 36–38.

16 Crone, J. A. (1997). Using Panel Debates to Increase Student Involvement in the Introductory Sociology Class. *Teaching Sociology*, 25, 214–218.

17 McKeachie, W. J. (1970). Research on College Teaching: A Review. Washington, DC: ERIC Clearinghouse on Higher Education.

18 Bowers, J. W. (1986). Classroom Communication Apprehension: A Survey. *Communication Education*, 35, 372–378.

19 Cohen, M. (1991). Making Class Participation a Reality. *PS: Political Science & Politics*, 24, 699–703.

20 Wade, R. (1994). Teacher Education Students' Views on Class Discussion: Implications for Fostering Critical Reflection. *Teaching and Teacher Education*, 10, 231–243.

6   Stay motivated

In this chapter, we're going to look at how you can build long-term motivations that can carry you positively through your studies. In the next chapter, we will look at ways to overcome short-term blocks on your motivation so you can get work done.

Barriers to motivation

There are a number of common barriers to staying motivated. The exact mix of barriers tends to be different for each student, but let's examine some of the major barriers that students tend to encounter.

Boredom

If you find something dull or tedious, it can be much more difficult to persuade yourself to engage with it. Even when you try, it may feel like your brain just somehow slips off the material. When school pupils are studying for exams, it isn't unusual to find some who spend more time on the subjects they enjoy and leave the subjects they find boring until the last possible moment. Making yourself focus on the boring stuff is hard – we can try to push ourselves through it, but unfortunately human willpower alone is weak and your brain likes to be engaged with things it finds interesting and pleasant [1]. In Chapter 4, we discussed some ways you can try to find an emotional or intellectual connection with a subject that you initially find boring. It's worth experimenting with some of these techniques rather than trying to force yourself through the boredom.

Anxiety

Anxiety can often present as a lack of motivation. This is partly because of the way the cycle of anxiety can work. Let's take an example – you have an assignment due in a few weeks' time. You are worried about this assignment, as you aren't sure you can do it well enough to get the grade that you want. Each time you think about it, you feel anxious. Anxiety is actually a kind of pain, and as a species we are programmed to avoid pain [1–3]. So, you find a short-term strategy to avoid the anxiety pain – you stop thinking about the assignment, pretend it doesn't exist and distract yourself with something else. Hey presto – the anxiety feeling goes – for now! Over time, this practice of avoiding can grow and become a habit; as a result, you find yourself in the situation of wanting to do the work but at the same time not wanting to do it. By avoiding the initial anxiety, you can end up losing your motivation to complete any assignments at all. We've covered some approaches to address this in Chapter 3 and we'll look at some more in the next chapter.

Uncertainty

Sometimes, we aren't able to engage with something, because we just don't understand what we are supposed to do. If you don't understand what you are being asked to do for an assignment or how you should go about completing it (i.e., what method to use), then it is much more difficult to get going on it. This uncertainty can feel overwhelming and make trying to find a way forward like trudging through quicksand. As a result, your motivation seeps away. In these circumstances, it is often better to take a step back. Rather than trying to engage with the content of the assignment, get some clarity about what it is that you have been asked to do and how best to approach it. Then build a plan for how you can get from starting the work to submitting it on time. It may help if you seek advice from your tutor or peers. When you are clear on what you need to do and how you are going to do it, you can begin to work on the task.

Habit

As human beings, we like routine and pattern. We often fall into habitual behaviour without realising, and this can either help us be productive or rob us of motivation. If your daily routine includes hours of inactivity and you study or do academic work only when a deadline or test is almost upon you, it will be much more difficult to make yourself work when you need to. Alternatively, if you do academic work regularly and frequently (even if only for a short period of time), it is much easier to maintain motivation.

Competing priorities

Sometimes, an apparent lack of motivation is actually just an appropriate allocation of your resources. If you are a student with children, for instance, it may be that there are times when your academic studies are not the main focus of your attention. This is perfectly understandable and doesn't in any way mean that you don't care about your studies or that you won't be successful. At times like this, accepting the situation and taking a more strategic approach to your academic work make perfect sense.

However, there can also be times when we unwittingly have competing priorities that don't deserve to pull us away from academic work to the same extent. For example, computer games, social media, TV or streaming services can become addictive and so pull our attention away from our academic studies. Habits like these can rob us of motivation to do anything else – not just studying. To take control of this, it may help to begin by mapping out your typical day so you can see just how much time you are spending on these activities. Seeing and understanding the true picture can be a helpful first start. Then make a plan to change the pattern of your day – if you know there is a particular habit that is likely to suck you in, set yourself a rule that you aren't allowed to engage in it until you have done the things you need to do. When looking at the things you need to do, include academic work, exercise, eating well, sleep and fresh air.

If you find yourself in this situation and find it difficult to change, it may help to access some support, such as counselling, to help you alter these behaviours.

Feeling tired or lacking in energy

If your physical wellbeing is low, it can also be difficult to find the motivation to work hard. Not only is it difficult to summon up energy when you are tired but it can also be more difficult to find enjoyment, pleasure or fulfilment in what you are studying. Regularly getting a good night's sleep, eating well, exercising and staying hydrated can help to boost and maintain motivation.

The importance of meaning, control and feeling competent

As we have discussed in previous chapters, if you care about the subject you are studying and feel that you have the skills and ability to perform well and that you are in control of the process of studying, then it is easier to perform well and maintain motivation.

All of these things can be worked on, and if you are struggling for motivation, it may be worth spending some time thinking about whether the problem is in one of these areas. It may help to ask the following:

1. Do I find this topic meaningful? Do I care about it or find it interesting? If not, can I make it meaningful to me?

2. Do I feel I have the skills and knowledge to study this subject and complete the work I've been assigned? If not, can I get help to build these skills or acquire this knowledge?

3. Do I feel in control of the process of studying? Do I feel I have the time, resources and space? Do I understand what I have to do? Do I feel in control of my own behaviours?

Types of motivation – intrinsic vs. extrinsic

Decades of research have focussed on two different types of motivation identified by Deci and Ryan: intrinsic and extrinsic [4, 5].

When we are intrinsically motivated, we do things for reasons that are internally important to us. We engage in an activity (e.g., studying) because we find it meaningful, pleasurable or satisfying in some way.

When we are extrinsically motivated, we do things for external reasons (e.g., because we want to impress other people or to meet some externally set target). Completing an assignment purely to get a good grade can be an example of extrinsic motivation. Buying material goods as a way of attempting to 'buy happiness' can also be seen as an extrinsic act.

When we think about how intrinsic and extrinsic motivation works for students, we might view it as described in the table below.

Intrinsic motivation	Extrinsic motivation
Seeks internal affirmation	Seeks external affirmation
Studying a subject because you care about it rather than for reward	Studying a subject because it appears to be valued by others and may lead to future reward or respect
Focus driven by the enjoyment, pleasure or fulfilment that come from studying your subject	Focus driven by the potential future reward available or the possible risk of failure
Engages in assignments in order to learn or develop ideas or understanding	Engages in assignments because doing so is a course requirement or to get a necessary grade (or both)

We all have a balance of intrinsic and extrinsic motivation. However, research has shown that students who are more intrinsically motivated learn more and to a higher quality. Intrinsic motivation has also been found to improve creativity and problem-solving.

Beyond this, individuals who are more intrinsically motivated in life are also found to have better wellbeing and mental health. This is because focussing on those things that are personally meaningful to us increases our sense of fulfilment and satisfaction with life.

As we have already discussed, if you have an internal passion for your subject, this can boost your learning and wellbeing. However, it may also be worth looking at other parts of your life as well. It can be powerful and life-enhancing to free yourself up from external judgements or perceived rules to focus on those things that you actually care about.

Pursuing wellbeing via things that you care about and that give you meaning helps you to meet your underlying needs and leaves you more in control of the things that make you happy.

Identifying what is intrinsic and extrinsic for you

The way we think and talk about our motivations can often give us a clue to whether they are intrinsic or extrinsic.

Intrinsic motivations more often lead us to want to be active and to do things because we believe in them. When intrinsically motivated, we tend to think and speak using terms like 'I want to do...', 'I believe...', 'I care...' and 'I am passionate about...'.

Extrinsic motivations more often lead us to want to have things – both in terms of having material possessions and in terms of recognition and public status. When extrinsically motivated, we tend to think and speak using terms like 'I should...', 'I want to have...', and 'I want to be...'.

Motivation and deep/surface learning

If you've been reading this book from start to finish, you may have noticed that there are significant similarities between the concept of intrinsic and extrinsic motivation and the concept of deep and surface learning that we encountered in **Chapter 4.**

This is because the two things are actually linked. Deep learners are more likely to be intrinsically motivated by their learning, whereas surface learners are often extrinsically motivated [6].

Meaning, pleasure and strengths

Working out what intrinsically motivates us requires a level of self-reflection. This isn't always easy, and it isn't surprising that many students can find it difficult. Society and schooling can often encourage us to focus on extrinsic motivations, like acquiring material goods, and so we never spend time thinking about what gives us personal meaning – or if we do we dismiss it as unrealistic or less important.

Harvard academic Tal Ben-Shahar created a model that can make this process of self-reflection easier; he calls it the MPS process. He sets out this model and the evidence to support it in his book, *Happier* [7].

Using this process, you will need to consider three questions:

1 What gives me meaning?
2 What gives me pleasure?
3 What are my strengths?

In my experience of using this process with students, it can sometimes take a while to come up with answers to these questions. To begin with, you may not be able to identify things that give you meaning. Some people also find it uncomfortable to spend time identifying their strengths. Nevertheless, it is worth persevering – the process of coming up with answers can in itself be good for your wellbeing. Recognising that you do have strengths can improve your self-perception and confidence, for instance.

If you are finding it difficult, it may help to frame or phrase the questions in a different way. For example:

1 What gives me meaning?

   You could also ask, what do I care about? What am I passionate about? What lights me up inside or makes me excited? What do I want to change in the world? When in the past have I felt a genuine sense of purpose?

2 What gives me pleasure?

   You could also ask, what do I enjoy? What am I doing when I feel at my happiest?

3 What are my strengths?

You could also ask, what am I good at? What do other people say I'm good at? When do I feel most competent and capable?

On a sheet of paper, make a list of answers to all three questions. To really get the most out of this exercise, it helps to go beyond the first few ideas that pop into your head. Spend some time really thinking about it – think about moments in your past when you have felt good, engaged and motivated and recall what you were doing at the time. The more things on your list, the better.

When you have three lists, you will probably find that some things appear on more than one of them. (Don't be concerned if this isn't obvious straight away; the way you've phrased things or thought about them can mask the fact that they are essentially the same thing.)

Let's take an imaginary student and list some of the things that give them meaning and pleasure and use their strengths.

Meaning	Pleasure	Strengths
Campaigning for the environment	Being with friends	Languages
Helping others	Painting	Playing tennis
Reading	Travelling	Painting
Understanding different cultures	Being in nature	Understanding other cultural viewpoints
Painting	Listening to music	Understanding ecology
Working with plants	Playing tennis	Cooking

Taking these lists, we can now begin to construct a Venn diagram to see where the overlaps are – checking each item to see whether it appears on another list in another form of words.

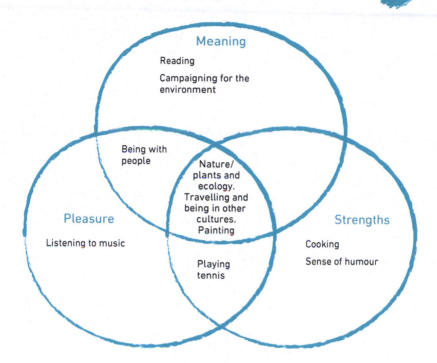

As you can see, a number of things have appeared in all three lists and some on two. We can see that the things that give this student meaning and pleasure and use their strengths involve travelling to and understanding other cultures, working with plants and nature and painting.

Having clarity about this, our student can then shape their studies, assignments and hobbies towards those things that appear on all three lists, choosing modules, courses and assignment questions that focus on one or more of these things.

The really helpful thing about the MPS model is that it can also help you think about the career and life you want in the long term as well. For our student, they might want to investigate careers that allow them to travel to other cultures, work in nature and/or use their artistic creativity. Having a clearer idea about your long-term direction, in this way, can help you to maintain your motivation. If you feel you are working towards a meaningful life and career, it can be easier to find the energy and enthusiasm you need. We will talk about this more in Chapter 12.

The importance of routine and structure

Understanding our intrinsic motivations and focussing on activities that give us meaning, pleasure and a sense of competence and achievement can definitely help to keep us motivated. However, alongside this, we need to be aware of the impact of our day-to-day routines and activities.

Humans are creatures of habit, and some habits can be more beneficial for us than others. Over the years, I have seen many students whose daily routines have stripped them of their motivation. Often, by the time these students get to me, they will have received a diagnosis of depression and may be taking medication. When we first meet, I spend a little bit of time getting to know them and how this experience is affecting them. As part of this, I often ask them to describe their day, and, for students in this situation, what I hear back often goes a bit like this:

> 'Well, I wake up at about 12 and maybe stay in bed for another hour. Then I get up and play computer games or watch Netflix for a few hours. Then at about 6, I'll have something to eat and talk to my friends, maybe have a shower. By then, the day is gone really and I've not done much. Again'.

The idea of having nothing to do can be seductive – imagine having all of your time to yourself, no pressure, nothing you must do and nowhere you have to be. It can sound wonderful. But the truth is, we aren't very good at doing nothing. As we discussed above, we need meaning and purpose in our lives and this requires structure and routine.

Living day to day, in the way described by the student above, is a recipe for low mood, low energy and low motivation. Having no routine or structure to your day can leave you feeling sluggish, lethargic, unmotivated and unhappy.

Of course, this isn't to say that the odd duvet day here or there can't be a nice break. As always, this is about balance – being too busy can also be bad for our wellbeing and sometimes, after a really busy period, we need the opportunity to recover. But duvet days should be breaks from routine – not an everyday event.

Creating helpful structure and routine

Building a routine that works for you generally takes planning and experimentation. Another thing that we, as a species, aren't great at is monitoring time as it passes. Our emotions can make time speed up or slow down – things that we enjoy feel like they go quickly, and things that are boring tend to go slowly.

So waking up in the morning and hoping that your time management will somehow work is something of a risk. It is far more effective to plan your time in advance. That way, when you wake up, you immediately know what you are going to do that day and can use that to propel you out of bed with a sense of purpose.

Remember, when you build a routine, it is important to try to meet your needs in balance. You will need breaks in the day and some time for fun and pleasure as well as time to study and attend class. You will also need to attend to practical things, like shopping for food or doing your laundry.

Over the page, you can find a planner that you can use to timetable the next few days. Below, I've also provided two examples of the kind of time planning I sometimes see that can trip students up. The first is the unplanned timetable.
(To be frank, I usually don't see this written down – it's just what happens for some students who haven't really planned at all.)

You can see that this student has drifted through the week, absolutely meaning to do some academic work but never quite getting around to it.

The over-planned timetable, on page 89, suffers from the opposite flaw. There is no way this student can possibly fit everything they've planned into the week. On a number of

The unplanned timetable

Name:

Calendar*pedia*
Your source for calendars

Time/period	Monday	Tuesday	Wednesday	Thursday	Friday
9.00–10.00				Ask friends if they've done any work	Sleep in and miss lecture
10.00–11.00	Some work, maybe, if I can persuade myself to do it	Stay in bed pretending I don't have work to do	Lecture	Panic because everyone else seems to be 400 weeks ahead of me	
11.00–12.00					Stare at computer screen
12.00–13.00					
13.00–14.00					
14.00–15.00					
15.00–16.00		Stare at computer screen			
16.00–17.00			I really am going to do some work now		Ring family\friends to talk about why I should give up
17.00–18.00				Give up – it must be me. I'm just not good enough	
18.00–19.00		Netflix			
19.00–20.00	Freak out because I haven't done any work				
20.00–21.00					
21.00–22.00					Watch satisfying videos on YouTube

The over-planned timetable

Name:

Time/period	Monday	Tuesday	Wednesday	Thursday	Friday
9.00–10.00	Go on a run, read research book	Volunteering	Seminar	Group project meeting	Lecture
10.00–11.00	Learn Mandarin	Study skills session		Volunteering	
11.00–12.00	Write assignment	Redraft assignment plan		Start writing assignment	
12.00–13.00	Group project meeting	Email project group members	Read journal articles		Library
13.00–14.00	Paid work – while there, read 3 journal articles	Visit museum	Babysit for friend while typing up notes	Help friend carry art work to studio	Gym
14.00–15.00			Tutorial	Upgrade phone	Write up group work notes
15.00–16.00		lecture	Buy birthday present for friend	Work on society event	
16.00–17.00	Library – find 8 books, meet friends, email lecturer		Go for a run	Coffee with friend – birthday present	Paid work
17.00–18.00	Type up lecture notes	Call home while tidying room	Do laundry and sort bank account		
18.00–19.00	Help friend with her projects	Research	Design website	Seminar	Work on assignment
19.00–20.00	Plan next assignment	Student Union society meeting	Prep for group work		
20.00–21.00	Meet friends	Event planning	Search for summer work	Watch free webinar	Friend's birthday party

occasions, they're trying to do two things at the same time. They've also set a number of traps for themselves:

1   They haven't allowed time to move from one activity to another – we usually need some time to move physically from one place to another, reset our minds and possibly freshen up.

2   There is no room for the unexpected – they've allowed themselves no buffer room to absorb life and the reality that we can't predict every moment of every day.

3   They are going to be exhausted as they've left themselves no time to rest, take breaks or eat.

Generally, what happens when we try to maintain a schedule like this is that we become overwhelmed, then frustrated that we aren't keeping to our plans and eventually lose motivation because it all feels too much.

Use the planner over the page to plan out your next few days. Here are a few things to think about when doing so:

1   If it doesn't fit comfortably onto the planner, it probably isn't going to fit into your day. Be realistic and reasonable with yourself.

2   Using a planner sometimes makes us think in concrete blocks of time. For instance, we might plan everything in hour-long sections. You can be more flexible than this to accurately reflect how long you want to give to each activity: 1 hour, 2 hours or 5 minutes.

3   Think about when you personally are at your most productive and try to plan in study time during this period.

4   Pay attention to how you are balancing your time over each day and over several days – some days may be busier than others, and that is perfectly ok as long as you have recovery time allocated on another day. If possible, mix tasks to help you stay fresh.

5   Give yourself some buffer time to absorb the unexpected.

6   Be flexible – if you don't manage to keep perfectly to the timetable, that isn't a reason to give up completely. We have to allow for life to happen and for ourselves to be human. Achieving a balance in your time is another skill that will develop and improve the more you practice.

7 Remain open to unexpected possibilities – it may not be on your planner but if you get the chance to do something that will be good for you, your wellbeing or your learning, it is ok to alter your plans. But having a plan will mean you will know what you may have to compensate for later.

If you don't like using timetables to plan

As with everything else, nothing works for everyone. Some people just don't like working with timetables. However, that doesn't mean you won't benefit from planning some of your time in advance – you may just need to use a different method. Here are a few other options you may like to try:

- **To-do lists**

  Some students find it helpful to spend time each evening compiling a list of what they want to get done the following day. This ensures that you still have some direction and purpose to the day but allows you to feel a bit freer about the order in which you will do each thing. The same caveats apply here though – if your list is so long that you won't possibly get everything done, you may be setting yourself an unhelpful trap. It might also help to keep a balance of activities on your list – include work, study, socialising, fun and so on.

- **Mind maps**

  If you are more visual in the way you like to work, you may find it helpful to use a mind map to plan out your time. You can use images or colours to indicate priorities and add thoughts about what you might need for each activity.

- **Your phone**

  Most smart phones have diary apps, and you can download planner apps to help you plan your time. Having your day planned out on your phone can be particularly useful, as it will prompt you with regular reminders of what you had planned. This can be helpful if you are someone who tends to forget where they are supposed to be.

Weekly Planner

Time	Mon	Tues	Wed	Thurs	Fri	Sat	Sun

Build momentum and stay motivated

Research into motivation and psychology has identified a number of strategies that can help you to be more motivated. These strategies can be particularly helpful when attempting to change habits or adopt more healthy behaviours as a regular part of your lifestyle. You might like to experiment with some of these.

Recruit allies by telling everyone your intentions

Relying solely on our willpower to bring about change (like studying more regularly or giving up smoking) is something of a risk. If we feel tired, irritable or distracted, it is easy for our willpower to be overwhelmed and so we tell ourselves that 'we'll start again tomorrow'. Recruiting back-up for your willpower, in the form of people close to you, can help you to stay more motivated. This can work in two ways. First of all, if you recruit supportive allies, they can encourage you when you are flagging and praise you when you succeed. The second factor is that instinctively we don't like to be embarrassed. If you tell people that you are changing a behaviour and prompt them to ask you about it, you will want to be able to report back that you have been successful and true to your word. This outside pressure can help to keep you on track.

Using transition points to reset

We are creatures of habit. However, these habits often are cued by things in our environment that become part of the habitual pattern. If, when you get home every day, you immediately put on the TV and take a packet of biscuits out of the cupboard, then the simple act of walking into your home will trigger you to do this automatically. In effect, your brain thinks 'Oh, we've just come home, I know what happens now' and guides you to that behaviour.

This means that you can take advantage of anything that changes your normal day-to-day patterns to create new routines that your brain will associate with the new environment [8]. For instance, if you've just moved from home to university, immediately starting with the behaviours you'd like to adopt will create a new healthy habit associated with your new accommodation. Once you've established this pattern for a few weeks, your new surroundings will trigger you into the new healthy behaviour without your having to think about it or expend any effort persuading yourself to do it.

Useful reset points can be the start of a new term, a change in timetable, a change in accommodation, a new job or the start of a new year.

Temptation bundling

If you pair something you aren't keen on but know you should do with something that you do enjoy, then it can be easier to motivate yourself to do the thing you don't enjoy [9]. For instance, let's imagine you are someone who doesn't like exercising but loves a particular TV series. If you set yourself a rule that you can watch new episodes of the TV series you love only while you are exercising in the gym, then you will be more motivated to go to the gym. Over time, this association will also help you actually enjoy the gym more. You might apply this to studying by allowing yourself to listen to your favourite music or allowing yourself your favourite snack only when you are working.

Further reading

Motivation

Ben-Shahar, T. (2008). *Happier.* London: McGraw Hill – The Observer.

Deci, E. L. & Ryan, R. M. (1985). *Intrinsic Motivation and Self-Determination in Human Behavior.* New York: Plenum Publishing Co.

Deci, E. L. & Ryan, R. M. (Eds.). (2002). *Handbook of Self-Determination Research.* Rochester: University of Rochester Press.

Money and wellbeing

Sandel, M. J. (2013). *What Money Can't Buy.* London: Penguin.

Wilkinson, R. & Pickett, K. (2010). *The Spirit Level.* London: Penguin.

Meaning

Esfahani Smith, E. (2017). *The Power of Meaning.* London: Rider.

References

1   Steel, P. (2007). The Nature of Procrastination: A Meta-Analytic and Theoretical Review of Quintessential Self-Regulatory Failure. *Psychological Bulletin*, 133, 65–94. doi:https://doi.org/10.1037/0033-2909.133.1.65.

2   Tice, D. M. & Baumeister, R. F. (1997). Longitudinal Study of Procrastination, Performance, Stress, and Health. *Psychological Science*, 8, 454–458.

3   Kaftan, O. J. & Freund, A. M. (2019). A Motivational Perspective on Academic Procrastination: Goal Focus Affects How Students Perceive Activities While Procrastinating. *Motivation Science*, 5(2), pp. 135–156. doi:https://doi.org/10.1037/mot0000110.

4   Deci, E. L. & Ryan, R. M. (1985). *Intrinsic Motivation and Self-Determination in Human Behavior*. New York: Plenum Publishing Co.

5   Deci, E. L., & Ryan, R. M. (2002). Self-Determination Research: Reflections and Future Directions. In E. L. Deci & R. M. Ryan (Eds.). (2002). *Handbook of Self-Determination Research* (pp. 431–441). Rochester: University of Rochester Press.

6   Postareff, L., Mattsson, M., Lindblom-Ylänne, S. & Hailikari, T. (2016). The Complex Relationship Between Emotions, Approaches to Learning, Study Success and Study Progress During the Transition to University. *Higher Education*, 73(3), 441–457. doi:https://doi.org/10.1007/s10734-016-0096-7.

7   Ben-Shahar, T. (2008). *Happier*. London: McGraw Hill – The Observer.

8   Verplanken, B. & Roy, D. (2016). Empowering Interventions to Promote Sustainable Lifestyles: Testing the Habit Discontinuity Hypothesis in a Field Experiment. *Journal of Environmental Psychology*, 45, 127–134.

9   Katherine, L. M., Minson, J. A. & Volpp, K. G. M. (2014). Holding the Hunger Games Hostage at the Gym: An Evaluation of Temptation Bundling. *Management Science*, 60(2), 283.

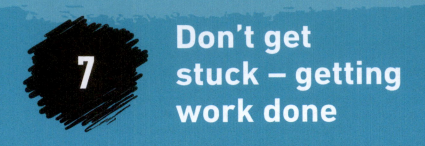

Don't get stuck – getting work done

Sometimes, starting or completing a piece of academic work can seem difficult, perhaps even impossible. You might want to get it done, you might want to produce a good piece of work, you might hope to get a good grade and yet you still can't bring yourself to start or complete the work. This can be a frustrating experience, and you might even find it perplexing – why can't you make yourself do something you want to do and know you need to do? However, it is a very common and understandable problem, and there are ways to overcome it. We're going to explore these in this chapter.

Where students get stuck

There are a few places where students generally get stuck when working on an assignment [1].

1 **You don't start – procrastination**
   We described this process in the previous chapter – because you worry about the piece of work, feel overwhelmed by it, bored by it or are uncertain about how to do it, you avoid starting it [1]. In other words, you procrastinate, promising yourself you will start it later but never managing to quite get round to it or, if you do, starting it too late to do yourself and the work justice.

2 **You start but get lost in the preparation – over-reading**
   Sometimes, there are positive reasons that cause students to get so absorbed in the research and discovery phase of a project that they get lost and so miss the deadline. As we discussed in **Chapter 4,** delving deeply into a subject is good for you and your learning but,

as we saw, you get maximum benefit if you couple this passion with organisation.

Sometimes, anxiety can also play a role in causing us to over-read. It can convince us that we don't know enough to do the work – no matter how much we actually know or how much we need to know for this assignment. For instance, it may try to tell you that, unless you know everything in the world about a particular subject, there is no way you can be ready to write a 1000-word undergraduate essay on it. This is obviously false but it can be very convincing in the moment, keeping you locked into more and more reading.

Or it may be that reading feels more comfortable than actually starting on producing work. By constantly reading, you are convincing yourself you are working – but you are actually procrastinating and avoiding the next stage of the task.

3 **You try to produce work but go blank – writer's block**
Although we call this writer's block, it can apply to all assignments – including scientific problems, creative art, mathematics and writing. Classic writer's block is that experience of sitting down in front of a screen or piece of paper (or standing before an easel) ready to do some work and then finding that nothing happens. Your mind may be devoid of thought or constantly distracted. You want to work but can't find the thoughts or produce any content. You are, in effect, in a type of trance.

4 **You lose confidence part way through – loss of self-belief**
Almost everyone who attempts to solve problems, writes or creates has had the experience of looking back over some of their work and deciding that it just isn't good enough. In fact, this experience is a necessary part of the process of almost any piece of higher-level work. Even professionals who produce work that is lauded by the public go through this regularly. The problem comes only when anxiety, low mood or self-doubt is able to hijack this experience. When this happens, rather than looking for ways to build on or improve what we've done, we might instead decide to delete it and start all over again or to give up completely.

5 You are unhappy with what you have done no matter how good – perfectionism

For some students, it doesn't matter how good their work is, they will still think it is not good enough. This can cause them not to submit good work, which would get high grades. If the work isn't perfect, they can't accept that it has any merit – this is why we call it 'perfectionism'. People sometimes regard perfectionism as if it were a positive trait – as though being a perfectionist meant being ambitious, wanting to perform highly and paying attention to detail. In fact, perfectionism is usually the enemy of ambition. It stops people from taking risks and learning new things and will frequently result in the individual's deciding not to even try something since they believe they cannot be perfect at it right away.

Creating new work is a process

Often, one of the things that can result in your getting stuck on a piece of work is that you fear the outcome. It might be that you are focussed on getting a poor grade or on how other people will judge you or on a concern that you can't produce a good-quality assignment. Continuing to focus on this fear will make it more difficult to engage with and complete the work. Therefore, it can help to initially move away from focussing on the outcome and focus instead on the process. By concentrating on the process, you can break the work down into more manageable and less scary steps and, by doing so, take control of your emotions and the assignment.

In my experience, no academic assignment, piece of writing or work of art appears fully formed in one go. I say this because I often meet students who seem to believe that they should be able to write an assignment in the same way that they read it. They should start writing with the first word and then produce each word, in turn, all the way to the end – every sentence and phrase should be perfect and in need of no revision. There may be one or two people in the world who can write perfectly like this, but to be frank, I don't really believe they exist.

Studies in creativity have identified a general process that most highly successful academics, researchers, scientists and artists work through [2]. It might seem unusual to think of academic work as creative – but problem-solving and creating new work, such as an essay or report, are at heart creative acts. Even the most scientific research involves creativity in designing new ways of examining questions, finding new solutions to problems and identifying new hypotheses. Learning is also a creative act – it is the creation of a new thought, idea or understanding in your mind that did not exist before.

Most creativity researchers agree that the creative process has two distinct phases: divergence and convergence.

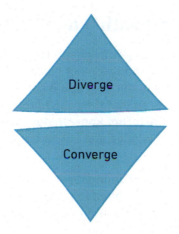

During the divergent thinking phase, you are conducting research, collecting information, generating new ideas, expanding your thoughts, making new connections and opening up multiple possible areas for exploration. During this phase, it helps to collect more thoughts and ideas than you need – some of these ideas probably will turn out to be dead ends or not as strong as you'd first hoped but this won't matter because you have generated more to draw on.

In the convergent thinking phase, the ideas and possibilities you generated are evaluated and then pared down, weaker ideas eliminated and problem-solving is refined. It is the process that turns your ideas into substance, and it is usually during this part that you actually produce work on the screen, page or easel.

The important point to notice is that to produce good-quality work, you will usually need to work through a process like this. We often make a mistake when we try to move from the narrowest point of the Diverge triangle straight to the narrowest point of the Converge triangle. It is like trying to take a 10-mile journey in a single step – and then assuming that the reason that you can't do this is that you are some kind of failure. Don't let anxiety or self-doubt convince you that you 'should' be able to do this – they are lying. Instead, let their voices drift to the back of your mind and focus on taking the first step forward.

Getting started with 'I don't know'

As we discussed in the previous chapter, recognising what you don't know is the foundation stone of learning. This can help to direct your research and thinking and it can also free you up from anxious thoughts so that they can't block your progress. If your job as a student is to 'not know things' and then learn so you are filling in these knowledge gaps, then not knowing something is not a problem.

You might want to start by noting down what you do know and understand and where you need to do more research and learning. If you aren't clear about what you do and don't know, use the retrieval practice technique we talked about in **Chapter 4** to help you.

Now plan

From here, it can help to actually plan out the process you are going to follow to complete this assignment. As with planning timetables, be flexible about this: life will intervene, and new ideas might mean you change your original plans. All of that is fine, but having a plan that gets you from this moment to the hand-in date can give you confidence that you can meet the deadline. Being able to tick off the steps you have already completed can also reassure you that you are making progress.

There are many ways to plan out a piece of work: some people like to work with minimal notes, and others like to plan in very close detail. If you haven't taken control of the process in this way before, you may want to experiment to find a method that works best for you. Remember, though, to plan time for every stage of the process – diverge and converge – don't leap straight to writing, painting or problem-solving. Let's look at an example.

Using a flow chart

The flow chart below sets out an example process that is focussed on the diverge stage of completing an assignment.

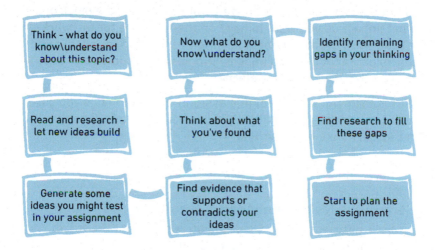

Here, you can see that this process starts simply with thinking. It can be easy to think of academic work as sitting at a desk, writing on paper or a screen. But, in fact, most academic work takes place in your head. Thinking is the crucial element in learning. Thinking about a difficult subject helps you to understand it better, thinking about complex problems helps you to find solutions and thinking about academic work helps you generate ideas, define an argument and structure your answers. Placing thinking at the centre of your work can help you improve the quality of what you do.

It also frees you up to be able to work in many places – you can think while going for a run, brushing your teeth or travelling on the bus. This can be useful if you have other commitments outside university and need to make the most of your time.

At this point, it can also be worth taking some of the steps we identified in this chapter and the preceding chapter:

- Identify clearly what you have been asked to do.
- Identify how you are going to do it.
- Identify reasons to connect emotionally to this assignment.

Then you can bring all of this together to generate some ideas about how you are going to tackle the question or problems you've been set. If this is a narrative piece of work, like an essay or a report, use this part of the process to decide what you want to write about and what story you want to tell. If it's a piece of art, what impact do you want to have on the audience for the work? If it's lab work, what is it about solving this problem or conducting this experiment that you think is important for knowledge or making the world a better place?

This is the point to connect this assignment with things you care about or are passionate about to provide a direction for your research, thinking and writing.

Generating ideas – enhancing creativity

It can be difficult to force good ideas to appear, but there are some things we can do to enhance our creativity.

Providing the right foundations

Research has shown that you are more likely to be creative and problem-solve successfully if you take care of your physical and psychological wellbeing (as we discussed in **Chapter 3**). Ensuring that you are hydrated, eating healthily, getting exercise and spending time outside will help you to think and generate ideas. Sleep is particularly important for creativity.

Incubation

The unconscious mind processes at a much, much faster speed than the conscious mind. What this means is that sometimes it can be helpful to let a problem or assignment task drift to the back of your mind while you do other things. Allowing a problem to incubate in your mind while not thinking about it will result in fuller processing [3]. Spend some time reading and thinking about the subject or question of your assignment and then move your focus onto something else. You may find new ideas bubbling through, or it may just be that, when you come back to the subject again, your thoughts have moved on.

Use mild distraction

One way to help the incubation process is to use mild distraction. This has been demonstrated by researchers using a version of something called the brick task. The brick task is a test of divergent thinking. Participants in this task sit in front of a house brick and are asked to come up with as many uses as possible for it in 2 minutes (using it as a paperweight, a doorstop, etc.). Unsurprisingly, some people are able to come up with more ideas than others.

Researchers have shown that what participants do after this task can have an effect on their creativity. For instance, let's say that after the first brick task all the participants were brought, one by one, to a table, on which had been set a pile of coloured building blocks. One third of the participants were instructed to simply sit at the table and do nothing. A second third were asked to arrange the blocks into different colours. The final third were asked to use the blocks to build a house.

After a few minutes, the participants were brought back in front of the house brick and asked to come up with a new list of uses for it. Research has shown that, this time, one of these three groups will be far more creative and will come up with more suggestions than the others. Can you guess which?

The answer is that the second group (those asked to arrange the bricks into different colours) will be more creative [4, 5].

For the group that is asked to do nothing, the problem will sit at the front of their mind, and so they won't get a chance to incubate. For the group asked to build a house, the task will be too cognitively demanding and leave no capacity for their unconscious mind to work on the problem. The group organising bricks into colours have just the right amount of mild distraction to allow the problem to slip into the back of their brain without overpowering their unconscious thoughts.

You can use this finding, when you get stuck on a problem, by identifying things you can do to mildly distract yourself. This might be simple household tasks like taking clothes out of the washing machine or putting away washed dishes. Just be careful that you don't become so absorbed in cleaning up that it becomes procrastination. Keep the task short and then bring yourself back to the work.

Do something in an unusual way

As we have already discussed, human beings are creatures of habit, and habits can lead us into routine thoughts and patterns of behaviour without our even realising. For this reason, old habits can actually keep us stuck in old thought patterns and block new ideas. Researchers call this 'functional fixedness' [6]. This means that your thoughts are fixed into one rigid way of viewing or thinking about something. In contrast, generating new ideas requires cognitive flexibility – the ability to let go of old thoughts and ideas to produce something new.

One of the ways in which you can move your brain out of this stuck feeling is to surprise it by taking something that is usual and changing it in some way. For instance, in one study, researchers showed participants a video of someone making a sandwich – one group saw a video of someone making a sandwich in the normal way, and the second a video of someone making a sandwich in an unusual way. The participants who watched the second video were able to generate more creative ideas immediately afterwards [6].

By scrambling previously rigid thought patterns, you can free your brain up to generate new ideas. Experiment by taking something you do regularly and do it in a different way (e.g., putting milk in a bowl and then breakfast cereal, sitting at the wrong side of your desk or changing your morning routine).

Go for a walk

There is a long history of people solving problems or coming up with new ideas while walking, and research shows that walking increases creativity and boosts your wellbeing. If you get stuck on a problem, take it for a walk and by the time you get back you may well have solved it [7].

Listen to positive music

Music has the power to change our mood and to have an effect on our thinking ability. Research has shown that listening to 'happy', uplifting music can enhance your ability to generate new ideas and think creatively [8].

Treat new ideas like babies – weak when just born

Just before we have a new idea or insight, the part of our brain that acts as a censor gets shut down. To allow new ideas to be born and develop, we have to protect them from harsh criticism. Whenever you have a new idea, don't rush to evaluate it and see whether it's a good one. Note it down and give it time to develop and grow in your mind. Most new ideas have flaws, but if you work to strengthen them, some of them will develop and be worth pursuing. If you crush every new idea immediately because of any weakness you find in it, then few of your ideas will ever see the light of day. Accept the weakness of the idea but hold onto it for a while and see if you can build on it.

Take control of procrastination

As we have already discussed, it can help to break an academic project down into smaller chunks or steps so that it feels more manageable.

Equally, it can help to break down your work routine into smaller, manageable blocks of time. If you intend to sit and work for 3 hours straight, you may well find yourself dreading the experience and so avoiding it. If you are finding it difficult to overcome procrastination, start with smaller blocks of study time. Promise yourself that you will work for 15 minutes. If, once you get started, you find that everything is flowing and you can keep going for longer – that's great, keep going. If, on the other hand, you manage only 15 minutes, at least it's 15 minutes more than you would have done. What's more, because you've made a start, it will probably be easier to do another 15 minutes tomorrow. As this becomes easier each day, you can gradually increase the amount of time you are working. It's also worth remembering that sometimes it can be possible to complete an assignment by working in short, intensive bursts.

Whatever you manage to do – celebrate it. Anxiety and low mood may want to make you focus on what you haven't done. In this way, they can demotivate you and, as a result, make you less likely to work tomorrow. Focus on the fact that you've done something, however small. You've taken a step forward and can continue to build on that. It may help to allow yourself a small reward if you manage to stick to your plans each day.

Take control of over-reading

At university level, it is generally not possible to know everything about any single subject. Even world-renowned experts will admit to not knowing everything about their area of expertise. Having a good depth of knowledge will help you to perform better on an assignment, but you also have to work with the reality of what you've been asked to do.

If you have a deadline for finishing a piece of work, there will be a point at which you must move on from researching to writing (or painting, problem-solving, coding and so on, depending on your discipline). This is one of the advantages of planning out a process for completing an assignment. You can use your plan to identify a date when you have to move on from the research to actually producing work.

You may want to begin by reading fairly widely to help generate ideas about what you want or need to do. Then, as you become clearer about what you want to say or need to do, you can become more targeted in your reading.

Once, you've entered this targeted reading stage, you can become very discriminating about how much you read – you can read just a relevant chapter rather than the whole book. Or you can use an abstract to decide whether you need to read a whole article. If you start reading something and realise it isn't going to be useful right now, put it to one side. If you want, you can come back and read the whole thing later, when you've submitted your assignment.

Remember to keep notes about what you find – it can be very frustrating when you're writing to know that you've read something relevant (which could support the case you are making) but you can't remember where you read it. Work with these notes to build your evidence and your understanding and to structure your assignment.

Take control of writer's block

Have you ever had the experience of sitting down to work, going blank and then looking up to find that time has flown by and you've done nothing? Or of staring at the screen or page, desperately trying to make your brain work?

This is something students and many others have experienced – probably forever. There are, however, some ways out of this – we looked at a few general ideas in the section on enhancing your creativity (above). Now let's look at some specific practices that can help.

1 **Warm up before you start**
   Writing at university level is a complex task. Moving from not thinking about academic work to writing fluently is a big jump in activity for our brains. In fact, it's often too big a transition to be able to accomplish quickly. Our brain needs an opportunity to build up to complex thinking and creativity. This is why we often switch on our computers, stare at the screen and find no words or solutions appearing. We haven't given our brain the chance to prepare.

   Coupled with this, computer screens can be hypnotic, putting us into a mild trance. Added to this, the internet offers us a number of easy-to-absorb distractions. Before we know it, we're liking pictures of someone's breakfast on Instagram and time is moving on.

It can help to switch on your computer and then step away from the screen completely. Use this time to warm up your brain to be ready for the task. Spend some time thinking about what you want to start work on today. For instance, if it's working on an essay, think about the first sentence or paragraph you will write. If it's a piece of art, think about the section you want to work on today and how you plan to do that work. Once you have the first idea clear in your head, sit down and start to work. Get that first idea down and it will be easier to maintain momentum.

It can help to think about working as you would think about going to the gym. You wouldn't start lifting heavy weights and undertaking the most strenuous exercise right away – you would warm up, get your muscles ready for the task and then go to work. Give your brain the same respect if you want it to do the heavy lifting of academic work.

2   Don't force it

If you go blank or the ideas just aren't coming, trying to force the answers out of your head can actually make it more difficult to move on. Remember in Chapter 3 we talked about how anxiety reduces our ability to think. Trying to force yourself when the work isn't coming can put you into an anxiety loop – you notice you've gone blank or have dried up, this makes you anxious or frustrated, which further reduces your ability to think, which makes you more anxious or frustrated, and so on.

If you go blank, take it as a message from your brain that you need to change activity. Maybe you need a break or a drink or something to eat. Just stepping outside for a few moments can help restart your thinking. Move away from your work, breathe, calm down and then begin to think about the work again. Don't sit back down or return to the work until you have a clear idea in your mind about what you are going to write or do next. (But don't let this become a form of procrastination – once you are calm, re-engage your mind with your work and once you have an idea, get back to your desk/easel, etc.).

3 Move

As we said above, writer's block is a kind of trance. Sitting still can help to keep you locked in this trance and prevent you from being able to work. Moving away from your desk, going into another room or stepping outside can help to re-orientate your brain and bring it back to life. Some students may even find they benefit from dancing or going for a run or walk.

4 Create a routine that gets you in the zone

Humans naturally form habits, and you can use that fact to create a routine that triggers your brain into an academic state of mind. Our brain uses something called association to switch on particular ways of thinking and feeling. It associates one thing in our environment with a way of feeling or behaving – so doing something regularly, before you do academic work, can trigger you into an academic state of mind. You can use music, reading, mindfulness practice – even making yourself a drink in a particular way just before you start work (and only then, so your brain associates it with work). Experiment and see what helps to build you into the right frame of mind.

5 Change the way you are approaching the work

If trying to make words appear on a screen, pictures to appear on an easel or equations to appear on paper isn't working, do something else. It may help to break down what you are doing or think about it in a different way. For instance, if you are working on a report or essay, it may help to use some mind maps or pictures to set out what you want to say or how you want to work. Or it may help to start on a different section. (Is it easier to write the Discussion rather than the Introduction?) Or maybe writing out by hand will help to get you started. Or writing in note form rather than full sentences. Or maybe you could try working in a different room or outside. The key is not to keep trying to push yourself through the block; instead, look for ways to ease around it.

Take control of self-belief

The way in which you approach your work can have a significant effect on your ability to maintain confidence in yourself and what you have done. If you expect to be able to produce work perfectly, straight away, you will inevitably be disappointed and leave yourself vulnerable to becoming anxious or down about what you have done.

If, on the other hand, you accept that academic work at university level requires drafting and redrafting to get to the required standard, then it will be easier to accept the flaws in your work and to see them as just areas for improvement. Academic work is a process of redrafting. Most of the academic papers that you will read in peer-reviewed journals will have been through at least a dozen drafts and quite often many more. Drafting makes your work better – it also takes the pressure off, particularly in the early stages of a piece of work.

This also applies to assignments that aren't essays or reports. Artistic work, design, problem-solving and lab-based research are all iterative – they build in iterations, one layer on top of the other. In this way, you also build your learning in layers and by the end of the assignment you will understand the subject much better.

In general, you should use the first draft just to help you get your ideas down in some sort of structure. No one should ever see your first draft. It is just for you and therefore it doesn't matter if it doesn't all make sense, isn't properly referenced or has obvious weaknesses. No one else will ever see it, so no one else will ever know.

If your tutor asks to see a first draft, give them your second draft and tell them it's your first draft. Free yourself up and give yourself permission to write something that might not be good enough for you to submit as a completed piece of work. Once you have a first draft down, you can start to improve it. Bit by bit, draft by draft.

You should also be aware that your mood will shape how you judge your work. If you are feeling down or unhappy with yourself, you will generally be a much harsher critic of your work and will be more likely to ignore what you've done well. Be careful not to let how you are feeling lead you to delete or scrap work. Try to save versions of what you have done and don't do anything dramatic with your work if you are in a low or angry mood.

Take control of perfectionism

Perfectionism is the enemy of ambition. This is particularly true of academic work at university level and above. Perfectionism will persuade you to be safe, to avoid mistakes and to try to deliver the assignment you think your tutor wants.

Perfectionism can also make you aim for something that isn't possible: the perfect piece of academic work. At this level, academic work cannot be perfect – even the greatest scientific breakthroughs have flaws and are subject to subsequent revision and new learning. If you read published academic papers in peer-reviewed journals, many of them have a section that describes the limitations of that paper and issues that may bring the findings into doubt. Brilliant, published academic papers are not perfect, and the authors themselves know this and highlight the paper's imperfections to the readers.

The fact that academic work is not supposed to be perfect is even baked into the words we use. The word 'essay', for instance, comes from the French word 'essayer', which means 'to try'. An essay is an attempt to discuss a subject. It is not supposed to deliver the perfect last word on a given topic.

It is important to remember all of this when perfectionism tries to persuade you to accept nothing less than perfection. If you accept perfection as the only acceptable aim, then when you realise you cannot achieve it, you will give up. In this way, perfectionism can persuade you to not even try.

This is not to say that you shouldn't aim to be ambitious. Wanting to be brilliant is absolutely fine. Be willing to challenge and stretch yourself – but be willing to fail every now and then and see this as part of your growth and development. The most brilliant academics frequently get things wrong, are able to admit it and use this learning to become even better academics. This is why we say that mistakes are a crucial part of learning.

Use your assignment to focus on what you can learn. Aim to be perfectly imperfect and you will give yourself the space to grow, learn and become a better student.

When your assignment has been marked, take time to celebrate your mistakes and to see them as the building blocks of your future learning. (We will talk more about this in Chapter 11.) Do also pay attention to positive feedback: if your tutor has taken the time to note which elements of your work are strong, it is worth paying attention to what they have to say.

Finally, sometimes, it can be easier to accept the flaws in your work if you separate yourself from it. Try to be your own best friend. When you look over your work, imagine what a best friend would say to you. What would they say was good? Where has your work improved? Is there evidence that there are things you know and understand much better now than you did before? What might they say about the quality of the work overall? Be kind to yourself – academic work is hard, and you can't know everything immediately. But if you allow yourself the time to develop, you will deepen your learning and you may even start to enjoy it more.

Taking control when perfectionism strikes – another relaxation exercise

Sometimes, being able to demonstrate to ourselves that our thoughts are unhelpful or untrue can help us to break free from them. Thinking about the fact that academic work can't be perfect may help you to let go of perfectionist thoughts. But this isn't always the case – sometimes logic doesn't work. As we've already discussed, this is because, when we feel anxious, the logical part of our brain is switched off. When this happens, we need to calm down our emotions and refocus. We've already described some ways to do this (7/11 breathing, progressive muscle relaxation, going for a walk, listening to music, etc.). Let's look at another one: using focussed attention.

- Switch off all distractions if at all possible. This includes emails, your phone and so on.

- Find a comfortable place to sit and then place an object in front of you – it doesn't matter what the object is, but one that isn't emotionally significant for you would be better for this exercise.

- Now focus your attention entirely on that object. Pay attention to its colour and shape, the texture of its surface, the way light and shadow fall on it and any other details you can see.

- If your mind or eye line wanders, bring it gently back to the object and focus upon it again.

- If you feel yourself zoning out, again bring your attention back into an active state and focus it upon the object once more, looking for some new detail you haven't yet noticed.

- Try to spend at least 5 minutes focussing in this way – if you can, pay attention for up to 15 minutes. Scrutinise the object in detail, finding new aspects or shapes that you hadn't noticed before.

- Once you've done that, gently move your thoughts back to your academic work – you may find standing up or moving around helps your mind shift back to the work.

- Think about a particular problem or question associated with the piece of work – don't sit down to work again until you feel you have made progress and know what you want to do next.

Further reading

Creativity

Csikszentmihalyi, M. (1992). *Flow: The Psychology of Happiness.* London: Rider & Co.

Csikszentmihalyi, M. (2013). *Creativity: The Psychology of Discovery and Invention.* New York: Harper Perennial Modern Classics.

Procrastination

Tefula, M. (2014). *Student Procrastination: Seize the Day and Get More Work Done.* London: Red Globe Press.

Sirois, F. M. (2016). *Procrastination, Health and Wellbeing.* London: Academic Press.

References

1 Steel, P. (2007). The Nature of Procrastination: A Meta-Analytic and Theoretical Review of Quintessential Self-Regulatory Failure. *Psychological Bulletin*, 133, 65–94. doi:https://doi.org/10.1037/0033-2909.133.1.65.

2 Mednick, S. (1962). The Associative Basis of the Creative Process. *Psychological Review*, 69(3), 220–232.

3 Ritter, S. M. & Dijksterhuis, A. (2014). Creativity – The Unconscious Foundations of the Incubation Period. *Frontiers in Human Neuroscience.* doi:https://doi.org/10.3389/fnhum.2014.00215.

4 Baird, B., Smallwood, J., Mrazek, M. D., Kam, J., Franklin, M. S. & Schooler, J. W. (2012). Inspired by Distraction: Mind-Wandering Facilitates Creative Incubation. *Psychological Science*, 23(10), 1117–1122.

5 BBC. (2013). *Horizon* – The Creative Brain: How Insight Works: BBC2, 00:20 27 June 2013.

6 Ritter, S., Kühn, S., Müller, B., Baaren, R., Brass, M. & Dijksterhuis, A. (2014). The Creative Brain: Corepresenting Schema Violations Enhances TPJ Activity and Boosts Cognitive Flexibility. *Creativity Research Journal*, 26, 144–150.

7 Oppezzo, M. & Schwartz, D. L. (2014). Give Your Ideas Some Legs: The Positive Effect of Walking on Creative Thinking. *Journal of Experimental Psychology: Learning, Memory, and Cognition*, 40(4), 1142–1152.

8 Ritter, S. & Ferguson, S. (2017). Happy Creativity: Listening to Happy Music Facilitates Divergent Thinking. *PLOS ONE*, 12(9), e0182210.

8 Improving performance in exams

If you want to perform well in an exam, it helps to think about your preparation in two ways. The first, most obviously, is academic preparation. It is difficult to do well in an exam if you have not memorised and understood the core information being tested.

The second is the need to prepare yourself to perform over a sustained period of time. Exams, at university level, require stamina, as they usually last several hours. (In some cases, such as research-based exams, they can last all day.) This requirement to perform at a high level, for several hours straight, means you need to arrive for the exam rested with energy stores to draw on and be able to productively manage your emotions and thoughts. This is another one of those things that sometimes are easier said than done.

Don't worry if this is something you've struggled with in the past. It is perfectly possible to overcome exam anxiety and to improve exam performance in most cases. In this chapter, we'll take a look at some specific steps you can take that may help. If you are still experiencing problems after experimenting with these ideas, it may be worth accessing some additional support from a university counsellor or study skills advisor.

Thinking about exams

As we discussed in Chapter 3, thinking creates reality. This is especially true when it comes to exams. How you think about exams can have a significant impact on how you perform in them. If you are scared of exams and they cause you high levels of anxiety, then it can be much more difficult to perform well. If, at the other extreme, you place no importance on them whatsoever, then it can be difficult to motivate yourself to prepare for them, and as a result, you are, again, likely to underperform.

As with many of the other things we've discussed, balance is key. You are more likely to perform well if you view exams as potentially helpful to you (and maybe even enjoyable). For many students, however, this can feel like one hell of a stretch. That doesn't mean that it isn't possible to get there over time. But clearly, it isn't how many students think about exams initially.

Exam anxiety

Exam anxiety is a common experience, potentially affecting up to 40% of students, according to some estimates [1].

One important point to remember is that exam anxiety is not the same as the motivational nerves almost everyone experiences just before an exam. As we discussed in **Chapter 3**, there is a big difference between being stressed and being stretched – even though sometimes they may feel similar. The motivational nerves you feel before an exam can give you extra energy, focus and enthusiasm to help you perform well. Exam anxiety, by contrast, reduces your ability to think clearly, concentrate and retrieve what you have learnt and may make you want to run out of the exam room.

Therefore, motivational nerves are not something you need to worry about. Instead, you can view them as fuel to help you do well.

Students who experience exam anxiety do so because they view the exam as a threat to them in some way. Or more accurately, they view the outcome of the exam as a threat – a piece of paper isn't usually particularly scary, and if you came across an exam paper that you yourself didn't have to sit, it probably wouldn't make you anxious.

Generally, we become anxious when we focus on the possibility of failing the exam and what we think the consequences of that may be, whether that means failing the exam completely or just under-performing against the standards we believe we 'should' achieve. When anxious, you may find yourself focussing on the feeling of failure that you believe you will experience, how you think other people may view your failure and all of the ways that this failure will stop you from doing what you want in the future.

However, as we have discussed elsewhere in this book, these are anxiety-powered thoughts, which means they may not be based on reality and aren't necessarily true. Anxiety will try to get you to imagine the worst possible scenarios and consequences, convincing you of the likelihood of failure and how it will impact on your life forever.

Remember, fighting with anxiety often does not help – you just end up being anxious about being anxious (see **Chapter 3**). Start by accepting that the worry you are experiencing is because you care about the exam and want to do well. The anxiety is alerting you to the fact that you need to prepare for it.

Then you might like to try one or more of the following ways of working with the anxious thoughts:

1 **Dilute the thought**
   You can start to reduce the power of the negative thought by adding some positive ones into your mind. Of course, it is possible the exam might not go well but it's equally possible that it might go brilliantly. What would that look like? How would it feel? Imagine being in the exam room, feeling confident and in control and knowing that you are doing well. It doesn't matter if the positive thoughts you have aren't realistic – you are just changing the number of possible experiences in your brain, releasing some of the anxious pressure. So, if you want to imagine looking up as you finish your exam and seeing your favourite film star making eyes back at you, go ahead and enjoy it.

2 **Look for evidence**
   Because anxiety can hijack you into believing things that are just not true, it is worth looking at what evidence it has to back up its claims.

Sometimes when I'm working with a student who is anxious about an exam, we'll look at their worst fear (failing it) and then ask – so what? What would the consequences be if you did fail it?

The answer is often – well, I'd fail that module.

Then we keep going, asking, so what would the consequence of that be? Each time, the student identifies the next consequence that they think would befall them. The answers tend to go something like this:

> 'Well, if I fail the module, I'll fail the whole year. I'll have to drop out of university. I won't get a degree. I'll never get a decent job. My family will be ashamed of me. My friends will leave me behind. My life will basically be over'.

When we then pause and go back to what the consequences would actually be, we discover that it is usually very different – the actual consequence would be that the student would have to re-sit the exam. Annoying but not life-ending. This is how anxiety can take your thoughts and bend them so that you believe something that isn't true.

Ask questions like – how likely are you to actually fail? How have you performed on previous exams? If you did underperform, how likely is it that your friends or family would never speak to you again? How well prepared will you be this time compared with other occasions? In reality, what would you have to do in response to a poor grade?

3 **Check your own goals and expectations**
Often, students who experience exam anxiety actually perform very well but just feel that they 'should' have performed better. Check whether your expectations actually belong to you, or is anxiety setting you up to fail by making you believe that anything below an impossible-to-achieve grade is a disaster. Take some time out to think about what you actually need to achieve, what you would like to achieve and what would be an amazing result but really isn't necessary.

4 **Bring your thoughts back to what matters**
As we discussed in Chapter 4, the point of assessments is not to accumulate grades but to learn. Exams are a really

good way of bringing concentrated energy to your learning and building knowledge and understanding of your subject. Can you move your focus (even just a little bit) away from grades, to concentrate on how the exam can help you learn more deeply, so that you can carry that knowledge into the next stage of study or into your career?

5 **Identify what won't be affected**

An exam is just an exam – many aspects of your life will not be affected by whatever happens in the exam room. It is important to remember and pay attention to this fact because anxiety may try to convince you that it will destroy your entire life. It won't. Think about relationships, hobbies, interests and things you do for fun that won't change because of the exam. You might also like to think about your personal qualities that will still be the same; if you are kind, intelligent, conscientious, thoughtful, brave or enthusiastic as a person, this will not be altered by an exam.

Preparing for an exam

Whether or not you experience exam anxiety, it is a good idea to prepare for exams in a controlled and planned way. Remember, the purpose of your planning is not just to revise so that you have the necessary knowledge; it is also to make sure you arrive at the exam feeling good and with energy to draw upon to help you perform.

Most people will find that building a timetable covering the weeks leading up to the exam will help (you can use the timetable template on page 90). Plan which subjects you will revise, when you will revise them and also when you are going to see friends, exercise, eat, have fun and rest. You should also factor in any other commitments that you might have, such as paid work or caring responsibilities – there is no point in pretending that these do not exist. Be realistic and work with the time you actually have, not the time you wish you had; otherwise, you will just become frustrated and lose focus, when reality prevents you from sticking to your ideal timetable. Be flexible and focus on effectively using the time you do have; this might include time when you aren't at your desk. For instance, on the way to do the school run or on the bus into university, you could ask yourself questions and try to answer them in your own head. This form of testing is a very effective revision strategy (see Chapter 4).

Taking control of the revision period in this way can help you to feel more in control, and as you progress, you can use the timetable to reassure yourself that you are preparing and will be ready.

Revising effectively

In Chapter 4 we also discussed evidence-informed ways of studying effectively and a few methods that simply don't work. We often find that students who struggle with exams or who experience exam anxiety adopt ineffective revision techniques, like re-reading notes [2]. This can actually help to increase your anxiety or the feeling that you aren't able to do exams. If you use an ineffective learning technique, you will probably start to notice that the material isn't going in and sticking in your mind. As a result, you will feel less confident and more anxious. By contrast, if you study effectively and start to notice that you are getting to grips with the subject and that you remember and understand it more, your confidence will grow. Revisit the list of effective learning techniques in Chapter 4 and use them to devise your revision strategy.

Remember, as you go along, that you don't need to know everything to pass or do well in an exam. Don't set yourself the perfect goal of memorising every single fact, theory or process; instead, aim to improve your knowledge and understanding of the subject being examined. Measure your progress against how much you knew when you started to revise (not how much you think is left to know).

Remember as well that it is ok to work in short blocks. Revising for three 1-hour blocks can be more effective than studying for one 3-hour block [3]. If you are able to grab only short periods of time to revise (even if it's in 10-minute chunks), this can still be effective if you plan and use effective strategies and techniques.

It is also sensible to do some practice papers (if possible) so you can work on getting your timings right. There is no benefit to be gained from answering 40% of the exam perfectly and not answering the other 60% at all. Work out how much time you need to spend on each section and practise completing them under timed conditions.

Don't drift through the revision period hoping it will all come together. Plan, use evidence-informed learning techniques and pay attention to your progress and you will learn more and grow in confidence.

Preparing you for the exam

There are a number of steps that you can take to ensure that you are physically and psychologically prepared for your exam:

1 **The basics – again**
   If you are reading this book from cover to cover, you will already know that your diet, getting exercise, going out into sunlight and staying hydrated are important for your wellbeing and your learning. The point is still worth repeating (and worth repeating over and over – I'm perfectly happy to become boring on this point). Nevertheless, it isn't unusual for students to abandon good habits as they approach exams and to start snacking on sugar, reducing sleep and abandoning exercise. There is a certain logic to this – if you don't go to the gym, then you might be able to cram in another hour or two of studying. This seems to make sense except that we know that the exercise will help you to learn and maintain your stamina, both for the revision period and during the exam itself. It will also help you keep anxiety in check.

   Anxiety may try to use the upcoming exam to talk you out of your good habits – it may tell you that you 'should' focus on the exam and you don't have time for exercise. Remind yourself that exercising is exam preparation. Taking time out to cook and eat a healthy meal is helping you prepare for the exam. Stay in control and take care of your physical health, knowing that this will help you perform well.

2 **Don't abandon your hobbies**
   When planning your timetable, make space, if at all possible, to maintain your hobbies, whether that is playing a sport, playing a musical instrument or watching films. Your hobbies

probably play an important role in helping you to de-stress and give you something to look forward to each week. This helps you stay motivated, maintains your energy and keeps anxiety under control. We need time to have some fun and let off steam – especially when there are increased stressors in our life (like exams). Of course, it may be that you have to reduce some of the time spent on hobbies if you can't find enough time to revise otherwise. But don't give them up completely. Having some relaxation time, doing something fun and engaging with the world outside of your exams can help you retain a sense of perspective and come back to your revision with renewed energy and focus.

3 Sleep
It can be tempting to study late and sacrifice sleep, but as we've discussed elsewhere in this book, this will actually reduce your exam performance (see Chapter 3) – you will remember less, have weaker concentration, be poorer at problem-solving and have less stamina to last through the whole exam. During your revision period, pay extra attention to your sleep routines and be disciplined about giving yourself the best opportunity to get the sleep you need. Anxiety and nerves just before the exam may make it less easy to sleep, but don't worry about this unduly. If you've slept well up to that point and given yourself a big sleep window in the nights before, you will be rested well enough to perform.

4 See your friends
Being connected to others is one of our needs as human beings. If we deny ourselves the opportunity to socialise, it can have a negative impact on our wellbeing and learning (see Chapter 2). Obviously, partying during exams is likely to be a bad idea, but meeting up for a coffee, a walk in the park or a meal together will help you feel more connected, provide you with some outside perspective and help you let off steam.

5 Don't be tempted to cram at the last minute
Cramming at the last minute can reduce exam performance and doesn't lead to any improvement [3, 4]. The evidence on this is pretty conclusive. Don't let anxiety bully you into last-minute cramming; it won't help and will probably make you more anxious and sap your energy levels right before the exam.

But I crammed before an exam and got a question right as a result

This is a common objection from students when told that cramming doesn't help. It is a perfectly understandable objection. The student remembers a mark they picked up because of something they learned when they were cramming the night before the exam. Therefore, cramming helped. Unfortunately, we know this conclusion is wrong, but it is one that human beings are vulnerable to making – it is called availability bias [5].

In this circumstance, it is easy for the student to identify the mark they gained as a result of the cramming. Much less easy to see are the 10 marks they lost but would have gained had they been more awake, alert and rested [6]. This is why it is important to subject experiences like this to research – and the findings here are clear. You may learn something the night before that you would otherwise have missed, but you will lose far more marks as a result of being tired and having scrambled the learning that was already in your brain.

6 **Sort the practical stuff**
   When we are worried about something, we can neglect to sort out the basic practicalities associated with it. This can be particularly true of exams. This might be because you are so preoccupied with what you are studying that you simply forget to attend to the practical stuff. Or because you are anxious, you avoid thinking about practical arrangements since thinking about them makes the exam feel real and that feels uncomfortable. But avoiding or forgetting to sort this stuff out inevitably leads to a last-minute scramble that just makes you more anxious and distracted right before the exam, when you most need to feel together and focussed. Take some time in the days and weeks before the exam to make sure you have everything ready.

   Check what you will need in the exam (pens, rulers, calculator, clean copy of a book, etc.) and try to have spares wherever possible. If you are allowed to, ensure you have a bottle of water to take in with you so you can stay hydrated.

Make sure you know where the exam room is and how to get to it – don't assume you'll figure it out on the day of the exam. Trying to find a room when your adrenaline is flowing can make you feel more anxious, which in turn might make it more difficult to find the room, and so you enter an anxiety spiral. Walk the route to the exam room well before the exam so this isn't something you need to waste energy thinking about on the day.

The 24 hours before the exam

To maximise whatever preparation you've already done, it is important to pay attention to how you use the last 24 to 36 hours before the exam. If, on the day before the exam, you abandon good habits and party or overwork, then a lot of the good work you've done won't show in your performance. Even if you haven't done as much work as you would like or think you need, this is the time to really focus on getting yourself to the exam ready to perform and not on cramming in more studying.

Remember, anxiety likes drift, so plan the day out and make sure it is structured and helpful. You may want to work back from the time you would like to go to bed. What time will that be? When you've identified your bedtime, what could you do in the hour before that to relax and give you the best chance of a good night's sleep? It might also help to think about getting some fresh air and some exercise and planning to eat well during the day.

Any revision that you do on the final day should be short and concentrated. If you've made the most of your revision period, then at this point you are just reminding yourself that you are prepared and ready academically.

If your revision period has been disrupted or was not as effective as you would like, then revise in a targeted way in a few short bursts. In this circumstance, it makes sense to take a strategic approach. In what areas can you maximise your performance? Plan this out before you start to work and remember to use the effective techniques we've covered in earlier chapters. Then finish early in the evening so you can wind down and sleep well.

This will help to ensure that all the learning you've done will be consolidated.

The day of the exam

Again, be in control of your day. It might help to consider the following:

- Set an alarm to get you up out of bed with plenty of time before you need to leave home, so you don't spend the morning in a rush.

- Make sure you eat breakfast – if you find this difficult, eat something that is easy to digest (e.g., a banana) and make sure you rehydrate. You will benefit from having some food in your system to provide you with the energy you will need.

- Choose a playlist to listen to on the way in. Music can alter your mood, so don't leave to chance what you will be listening to [7]. Put together a playlist of music that helps you to feel good, relaxed, positive and in control.

- Do you want to spend the time before the exam with your friends or on your own? It is surprising how many times I ask that question and students tell me that they'd rather spend time alone but spend it with friends. Or that they'd rather spend the time with their friends but spend it alone. Do the thing that helps you most.

- Take some time outside, notice the air on your skin, focus on your surroundings (can you see trees or birds or flowers?) and use 7/11 breathing to help you stay calm and confident.

- Plan to get to the room in plenty of time so that you can walk there at a reasonable pace and don't arrive at a run.

In the exam

There are a number of common trigger points in exams that can spark a jolt of nerves through your system. If you accept this as normal motivational nerves, this will pass quite quickly. However, sometimes students experience these nerves and think 'Oh no, I'm anxious!', and by engaging with that thought, they genuinely become anxious. Instead, remind yourself that these feelings are normal and are probably being experienced by everyone who is sitting this exam. Breathe and let the feeling go.

So, what are these common trip points?

1 **The moment you are allowed to enter the exam room**
It may help if you don't rush to get into the room. Move at a gentle pace and keep breathing. Remember, the exam is not a threat to you and the room can't hurt you. You may even find that once you get going, you enjoy the exam.

2 **'Turn your paper over now!'**
Even decades after their last exam, that phrase can still make people feel a jolt of nervous energy running through them. It will usually help if you don't turn your paper over straight away. First, take a breath and let the nerves settle; then when you are calmer, turn the paper over. If you turn the paper over while the initial shock of nerves is still running, you may find it harder to take in the questions, which then can worry you and trigger more anxious feelings. Stop, breathe, feel calm; then begin.

3 **The first read-through**
Don't worry if on your first scan through the questions, your brain comes up blank. Again, this is very common and it doesn't mean you won't be able to answer them or perform well. Take your time and find one question that you can answer – depending on the type of exam you are doing, you may be able to take a moment or two to either answer it or plan out an answer. Now that you have momentum, you will probably be able to find more answers or be able to start building possible answers.

4 **Towards the end**
Sometimes, students look up at the clock and are surprised by how much time has passed. Don't let this throw you. If you haven't noticed the time going by, it probably means you were in flow and have been performing well as a result. If you've planned out your time, you will still have enough time left to

finish the paper. Remember – you don't have to answer every question perfectly. Use the time you have left to complete the exam to the best of your ability, giving the marker as many opportunities as possible to give you more marks.

After the exam

Before you do anything else, congratulate yourself for whatever you have done. Yes, you may want to improve next time but start by acknowledging what you have done and what you are pleased about. This doesn't have to be about the questions or the exam itself. It might be that you can be pleased with how well you managed the revision period. If you are studying with lots of competing demands, you may want to note how much of an achievement it is to have revised for and sat this exam and met those other demands at the same time.

Think again about whether you are better off spending the time immediately after the exam by yourself or with friends – which would actually help you more? If you want to spend time with friends, maybe you could help them by getting everyone in your group to identify one thing they did during the revision period or exam (or both) that they're pleased with.

All of this isn't to say that you shouldn't analyse your performance and look for ways you can improve in the future. It just makes sense to wait until the initial moments have passed and to begin by working from what went well. Otherwise, it can be easy to get dragged into looking only for the negatives, which will set you up for feeling anxious next time around. When you do come to analyse how you've done, try to focus on what you have learned and can build on for next time. Exams are never perfect, but we can learn and develop from the experience.

Finally, allow yourself a small reward for whatever you have done well. This doesn't have to be a big deal or cost a lot of money. It might be some time with friends or a trip to the cinema or letting yourself spend more time on a hobby or pleasure. Do something that you will enjoy and mark it as a payment to yourself that you have earned with all of your hard work.

Further reading

Becker, L. (2018). *14 Days to Exam Success* (2nd ed.). London: Red Globe Press.

Carey, B. (2015). *How We Learn.* London: Pan Books.

Cottrell, S., (2012). *The Exam Skills Handbook* (2nd ed.). London: Red Globe Press.

References

1 MacDonald, A. S. (2010). The Prevalence and Effects of Test Anxiety in School Children. *Educational Psychology*, 21(1), 89–101.
2 Culler, R. E. & Holahan, C. J. (1980). Test Anxiety and Academic Performance: The Effects of Study-Related Behaviors. *Journal of Educational Psychology*, 72(1), 16–20.
3 Carey, B. (2015). *How We Learn*. London: Pan Books.
4 Kornell, N. (2009). Optimising Learning Using Flashcards: Spacing Is More Effective Than Cramming. *Applied Cognitive Psychology*, 23, 1297–1317. doi: https://doi.org/10.1002/acp.1537.
5 Tversky, A. & Kahneman, D. (1973). Availability: A Heuristic for Judging Frequency and Probability. *Cognitive Psychology*, 5(2), 207–232. doi: https://doi.org/10.1016/0010-0285(73)90033-9.
6 Scullin, M. K. (2019). The Eight Hour Sleep Challenge During Final Exams Week. *Teaching of Psychology*, 46(1), 55–63.
7 Hodges, D. A. (2010). Bodily Responses to Music. In P. N. Juslin & J. A. Sloboda (Eds.), *Handbook of Music and Emotion: Theory, Research, and Applications*. New York: Oxford University Press, pp. 279–311.

9 Improving performance in presentations

We have known for many years that being afraid of speaking in public is notoriously common. A famous report from the 1970s [1] identified public speaking as the number one fear among Americans – putting it above death, which was number two on the list. As comedian Jerry Seinfeld pointed out, this means that at a funeral more people would prefer to be in the coffin than to give the eulogy.

In truth, the number of people who experience public speaking anxiety is likely to be much lower than this, and, most importantly, most people can learn to overcome anxiety and to speak well [2].

If you are someone who is confident speaking in public, then you can use this confidence to your advantage, but it is still worth taking some time to improve your skills and overall performance in presentations.

In this chapter, we are going to look first at anxiety, which is the most common barrier to performing well in presentations. Then we will explore some practical steps that you can take to improve the quality of your public speaking, whether you experience anxiety or not.

Why can public speaking make us anxious?

Even confident public speakers will often feel a few pre-performance nerves before they start to speak. As we've discussed elsewhere in this book, it is worth noting that these motivational nerves aren't the same as anxiety and can actually help by giving you energy to perform well. But the existence of these nerves tells us that, when we speak in public, we want to do well. Performing well when we speak in public is important to us.

This desire to perform well is a good and motivating thing, but if we allow our thoughts to slip to the dark side of wanting to do well, we end up focussing on trying to not do badly. If that thought gets hijacked by anxiety, we can quickly find ourselves thinking about exactly how our presentation might go badly and what the negative consequences of that might be.

There are a number of reasons why public speaking can make us anxious:

1 Social needs are under threat

When students describe what they fear from presentations, they often refer to feeling worried about being judged or humiliated. Humiliation is something that is acutely painful to human beings.

As we discussed in Chapter 2, we need to feel part of our community. This is such a deeply programmed need that even reading about it can be uncomfortable for some people. (If the next section makes you feel anxious as you are reading it, take a break for a moment, breathe and, if necessary, feel free to skip to point 2.)

Evolutionary needs theorists would argue that this goes all the way back to when we lived in the wild [3]. Then, our only way of surviving was to be part of a tribe. As an animal, we aren't particularly strong: we don't have a thick hide, we can't run very fast and we don't have sharp teeth or claws. On our own, we would be easy prey. What kept us safe was that we banded together to provide each other with protection. Being cast out of the tribe meant we were no longer safe.

Being humiliated can make us feel that we are being cast out of our tribe or group. It can feel like we are being judged and found wanting or that we are losing people's respect and that they like us less than they did before. In effect, it can feel like we are being ostracised.

If we allow these thoughts and feelings to take control, public speaking can feel like an enormous risk. Anxiety can convince you that if you give a presentation and it all goes wrong, you will be abandoned by everyone you know, no one will ever speak to you again and everyone in the world will know that you are stupid and incompetent.

Of course, all of this is a lie – but it can be very persuasive and seem totally reasonable in the moment. If you believe this lie, then giving a presentation can feel like a very risky and dangerous thing to do. We'll examine all of this a bit more below.

2 You feel you lack skills

Another one of the needs we discussed in Chapter 2 was the need for competence and achievement. Doing anything, if you don't know how to do it or feel incapable of doing it, can make you feel frustrated, anxious and incompetent. Having to do something that you don't know how to do, in front of other people, maximises these feelings.

Some research has shown that simply being trained to speak in public can significantly reduce people's anxiety. Just by increasing your skills, you can feel more confident, and so the anxiety ebbs away. There are some tips below to help you with this.

Of course, it may well be that you are actually very good at public speaking and have all of the necessary skills but still feel that you aren't good enough. This low self-belief can undermine confidence and lead to you becoming anxious. Training can still help you to recognise the skills you have and build on your ability so that you become more confident.

However, if you are someone who experiences this, it may help if you use some of the anxiety management techniques listed throughout this book. It may also help to work on your self-belief with a counsellor or therapist.

3 You've had a bad experience of public speaking

Sometimes, when something goes wrong, it can become imprinted on our minds. This is particularly the case if it was something scary, embarrassing or humiliating. If you've had an experience of speaking in public that you felt was awful and caused high levels of negative emotion, then it may be that it is the memory of this that is making you anxious.

In cases like this, therapy can be a real help. You might also benefit from gradually building up to a presentation in small steps. For instance, first you might present to one person whom you trust and feel safe with, then two or three close friends or family members and so on. The important thing when doing this is to ensure that the practice doesn't become another ordeal. Use 7/11 breathing (see page 23) to help you stay calm and begin with very informal presentations that are very short.

You might also like to try a visualisation technique – simply close your eyes and imagine the presentation going well. Imagine how this would feel, how you might grow in confidence, speak well and feel satisfied with what you have done. It doesn't have to be realistic; however good you think you are at speaking in public, let that drop away and in your imagination allow yourself to present really well.

The spotlight effect

Because we experience the world through our own thoughts and experience, it is easy to believe that everyone can see how we are feeling and what we are thinking or that everyone is paying attention to us at all times. In fact, most of the time, people aren't paying as much attention to us as we think – and they certainly can't see our thoughts.

In one study that explored this, individual participants (all students) were asked to wear a T-shirt featuring a picture of the pop singer Barry Manilow. (At the time, the experimenters judged him as very unfashionable and therefore wearing a T-shirt with his face on it was viewed to be very embarrassing.)

Each participant was individually escorted to another room where four to six other student participants were seated filling out questionnaires. These students were unaware that the real research was about their interaction with the student in the T-shirt.

Once the student in the Barry Manilow T-shirt had been in there long enough for everyone else to notice them, they were escorted back outside. Then they were asked to estimate how many of those seated in the room would recall who was pictured on their shirt. The participants significantly overestimated the actual accuracy of the observers (by a factor of 2). The T-shirt wearers were noticed far less than they suspected [4].

The truth is that people pay far less attention to us than we think. This is also true of how much you notice about other people. Most of the time, we have our own thoughts running in our head and are distracted by what has already happened that day, what we're anticipating happening later, daydreams, fantasies and worries. Also, we don't focus on just one person – even when we're engaged in an intense one-to-one conversation, our brain will continue to monitor the environment around us.

What all of this means is that people aren't scrutinising you in the way you might think. They can't read your thoughts and often will not notice or forget things that you say and do because they aren't particularly important or noteworthy for them.

This is important because often anxiety will try to convince you that small slips or stumbles in front of people will end your social life. If you stumble over a word, for instance, you might find yourself thinking 'Oh God, why did I do that? Everyone will think I'm incapable of even speaking. They will think I'm stupid. I'm so embarrassed; they probably don't even want to be around me'.

But by the time you've come to the end of that horrible thought spiral, the people around you will barely remember that the stumble ever took place. Why would they? It is of no real importance in their life – it isn't information that their brains will prioritise when deciding what should and should not be remembered from their day.

So breathe and let go – we all make stumbles and we all say daft things sometimes. It won't end your social life and it will cause you negative feelings only for as long as you focus on it.

So just how risky is giving a presentation?

In reality, it is very rare for any one presentation or speech to have a long-term effect on your life. Politicians may sometimes pay a price for a poor speech, but even in these circumstances, it is usually forgotten quickly as the news moves on. For the rest of us, speaking in public carries few real risks. In general, people aren't waiting to judge you harshly and are more likely to be forgiving than to want to see you humiliated.

The audience is on your side.

There is actually a good reason that explains why audiences are usually on the side of a speaker. As human beings, we are programmed to recognise and empathise with other people's pain [5]. When we see someone in pain, we feel a diluted form of that pain ourselves. This is caused by parts of our brain that are called 'mirror neurons' because they capture and mirror the emotion we see in someone else. This is why watching people laugh makes us smile and watching people cry makes us uncomfortable or sad.

When we watch someone speaking in public, we want them to do well since the alternative is watching a speech go badly – and when that happens, we experience some of the speaker's pain. If you've ever seen a comedian die on stage, you will know this. I used to be a stand-up comedian, so it's something I've seen (and experienced myself) many times. There is a moment when the audience suddenly realises that the comedian isn't going to make them laugh, and the whole room tenses up. You can almost feel everyone willing the comedian to find their rhythm and be funny. The audience finds the experience excruciating.

You can trust that whoever is watching is on your side because it is more comfortable for them if you do well.

If it's an assessed presentation – you won't be the focus of attention.

If you are in a class that requires you to give a presentation, then everyone else in your class will also have to give a presentation. That means that when you are speaking, their thoughts are probably going to be focussed on the presentation they have to give or, if they've already presented, on the one they've just done. The fact that you are all being assessed will also mean they will be even less likely to judge you harshly, as they won't want to be on the end of that kind of judgement themselves.

Everyone knows it's just a presentation.

Lots of people don't like speaking in public. If you don't like presenting, you won't be the only one in your class. This is something that most people understand. People also know that presentations are an unusual and slightly false phenomenon. As a result, a presentation usually won't change the opinions that your friends and classmates hold about you.

Ok, I get all of this, but I'm still not keen on speaking in public

Very often, when we speak in public, the thing that we fear is the emotion that we will experience while we are presenting. We are afraid we will be afraid. We worry about the feeling of being embarrassed – even if it won't last and no one else will remember it. As we've discussed earlier in this book, being worried about negative emotions can make us want to avoid them. Sometimes, students will choose modules or courses in an attempt to avoid having to give a presentation. This can deny you the opportunity to study a subject you'd find interesting, meaningful and otherwise enjoyable.

This desire to avoid can also send you on an 'I wish' thought spiral. 'I wish I didn't have to give a presentation. I wish I could get out of it. I wish I didn't feel like this...' and so on. This pushes up your anxiety, and you become more and more nervous about the presentation you have to give.

Instead, if you can, it will usually be more helpful to work on acceptance. Presentations are a fact of life. In most careers, there will be a requirement for you to speak publicly. It isn't something that can be easily avoided, and you don't want to let anxiety bully you into choosing careers you don't really want, just to avoid public speaking. This does mean that occasionally you might feel uncomfortable when presenting, but this uncomfortableness will not last and it cannot hurt you. It is just a feeling. Accepting it, working with it and letting it go will give you power over it.

But what if something goes wrong?

This is a fear that many students hold. What if the technology doesn't work? What if I forget something? What if I sneeze or cough?

The key is to home in on what the real problem is. Take a moment to think about that – if something went wrong during a presentation, what would the real problem be?

Things go wrong in presentations and performances all the time – but most of the time, we don't notice or we forget. The important element is your reaction. If you make a joke about it, apologise and move on, then no one in your audience will care. On the other hand, if you let it throw you and you lose concentration and flow, then it can derail your whole presentation. It's also worth remembering that if something goes wrong in an assessed presentation and you are able to retake control, you will impress your tutor and probably gain more marks – so embrace moments when things don't work. They are a chance to show your audience that you are confident and in control.

Speaking well in public

Speaking well in public is a skill. No one is naturally brilliant at it right away; it develops with conscious practice. This can be tricky if presenting makes you anxious because you probably want to do it and think about it as little as possible. However, if you take the time to practise, gather useful feedback, learn and develop, then you will find yourself getting better and more confident. In the next section, we'll look at some ways in which you can work on your presentations to develop your confidence and performance ability.

Before we look at that in detail, it is worth bearing one final thing in mind. If you can communicate, face to face, with one other person, then you have the innate skills to be able to present. We wrap the idea of presenting in lots of complicated thoughts and ideas, but essentially any presentation is just a conversation. If you've ever explained anything verbally (or using sign language) to anyone else, then you can present. The best presenters make you feel that they are having a conversation with you. Bearing this in mind can stop you from overcomplicating your presentation and can strip it of some of its scary connotations.

Planning and writing your presentation

The lessons from earlier in this book on preparing for exams and writing assignments apply equally well to presentations. Trying to maintain balance and looking after your wellbeing will mean that you have the resource to write and practise your presentation and to deliver it well on the day.

It will also help if you can shape the topic of your presentation so that you are speaking about something that you find interesting and important. This can help you to focus your work on sharing information and ideas that you think people should know rather than on delivering a perfect presentation.

There are also some specific steps you can take to make it more likely you will deliver a good presentation.

1 **Stick to the brief**

   Being clear on what you've been asked to speak about and how long you are expected to speak can ground your preparation in certainty and avoid last-minute panics. The length of time is particularly important. Enthusiasm, anxiety or uncertainty can drive you to overcomplicate things and prepare far more material than you need. Stay focussed and remember what this task is in reality. If you've been asked to speak for 5 minutes, then you need a brief introduction, two to three clear points that you wish to make, each with a very brief explanation, and a conclusion. There may be hours and hours of useful things that you could say on this topic but that isn't the purpose of your presentation.

Check the brief you've been given and, if necessary, ask your tutor or lecturer to clarify what you've been asked to do.

2 Focus your research

Once you are clear about what you've been asked to do, you can focus your research on the material you need to know. Remember, you do not have to be a world expert on the topic to be able to speak about it, and even world experts don't know everything. What do you need to know and what do you need to reference in your presentation? Keep notes and order them to help give you the beginning of a structure.

3 Identify your story

Every presentation is a story of some kind. Thinking about the story you want to tell will help you to come up with a coherent presentation and will make it easier for you to remember what you want to say. Stories stick in our minds better than facts. Having a story to tell will make it easier for you to deliver and easier for your audience to listen to and understand your presentation.

Like all stories, your presentation needs a beginning, a middle and an end.

In the beginning, you introduce your topic and the area you will be exploring. This is where you set the question that will drive your presentation – 'What is causing x?' 'How might we solve y?' 'What do we need to understand more?' and so on.

In the middle, you address this question with clear points. How much detail you go into at this point will depend on how long a presentation you are giving. But remember, this is a story. Don't just plan to recite a series of facts or theories. Make them talk to each other, build one idea on top of the other and make them flow. You can do this by setting up conflict – 'x says this but y says this and this causes us a problem'. Or by framing your points as part of one model – 'there are three elements of this problem that are important' – and then explaining how they link. Or by using a natural narrative flow if, for instance, you are discussing the life story of a famous historical figure.

In your conclusion, you want to draw all of what you have said together to deliver a clear message – 'all of this shows that...' Your conclusion doesn't need to be earth-shattering but it should draw together what you've already discussed into one or two 'take away' points for your audience.

4 **Write your script – but don't get too hung up about each exact word**

It can help to write out what you are going to say but this doesn't need to be scripted word for word. Writing a script to memorise in detail can be a trap – if you forget one word, you might panic and lose your flow entirely. Instead, it can help to write out the key points so you know the structure of what you want to say and how the story flows. This doesn't have to be using just words; you might want to add diagrams or pictures. Putting pen to paper can also help you to embed the presentation into your head.

Practising your presentation

There are a number of reasons for practicing your presentation. It can help if you practice in your head, out loud by yourself and with a small audience.

1 **Get your timings right**

Unless you've performed your presentation, there is no way to know whether what you've prepared is too long, too short or just the right length. Set a stopwatch and time yourself.

2 **Rehearsal aids memory**

If you practice your presentation several times, you are far more likely to remember it when you deliver it in the classroom. Remember, repetition is one of the ways we give things importance so they get coded into our long-term memory.

3 **Practising is part of the drafting process**

Practising the presentation will help you see what works and what doesn't. You can then redraft it and practise it again. In this way, your presentation will get stronger and will be easier to deliver.

4 **Practice makes your performance better**

The more you practise something, the better you get – however, it is useful to get feedback on your rehearsals; otherwise, you may be repeating mistakes without realising it. Find a tactful and honest family member or friend who will listen to your presentation and give you helpful feedback.

Delivering your presentation

In the previous chapter, we discussed ways of preparing yourself on the day of an exam. The same lessons apply here. Ensuring that you arrive at your presentation energized, well rested, hydrated and relaxed will help you deliver well. Try to avoid drinking too much caffeine beforehand as this can make you feel shaky.

There are also a number of techniques that can help you deliver your presentation well:

- Breathe. Use 7/11 breathing (see page 23) to help you stay calm and give you control over your voice. Breathe slowly and take your time.

- Speak so your audience can hear. Try to speak clearly and loudly – it's ok to be passionate but try not to speak too quickly for your audience to hear. Taking pauses every now and then can be a very effective way of resetting your pace and holding the audience's attention. It can also help if you vary your pace and tone, as this makes it easier for the audience to maintain concentration and follow what you are saying.

- Pay attention to your body language. There is no one way to look confident and in control. Some people like to stand still while they talk; others like to move around. Do what feels natural to you. But there are some general tips that do matter.

- Smile (when appropriate). This can help you feel better and put your audience at ease.

- Look up, so the people in the room can see your face and hear you clearly. If your face is hidden because you are staring down at your notes, it will be harder for people to feel they have connected with you and your message.

- Stand tall. This will help you to feel in control of your space and encourage your audience to believe you are confident (even if you are not).

- Decide what you are doing with your hands. Using your hands to emphasise what you are saying makes it easier for the audience to follow you. But if you aren't comfortable with this, it's ok to hold onto a lectern or have them clasped in front of you. If you are worried about your hands shaking, try to avoid holding your notes, as this will make you more aware of the tremor.

- Roll with anything that doesn't go perfectly. Remember, you are here to tell a story. If you forget one fact or miss out one thing you meant to say, it doesn't matter as long as the story holds together. No presentation is ever perfect; that doesn't mean it won't be good.

- Allow yourself to enjoy it. Sometimes, people who hate presenting go on to love it. If you find yourself enjoying a presentation, go with it. It doesn't mean you are a different person, it just means you've learned something new.

- Focus on your learning. When the presentation is done, think about what went well and then about what you'd like to improve. Remember, the purpose of this wasn't to do it perfectly. However it's gone, there will be positives you can take and build upon – don't just look for them in the presentation itself; also remember to think about what went well during the preparation and rehearsal phase.

One final thought – don't present as you

One of the most successful tricks to speaking well in public is to accept that this is a performance. That means that you won't speak and behave in front of an audience as you would in a one-to-one conversation with friends.

Instead, you deliberately decide to play a role. You are acting. You can imagine 'how would I perform if I were a confident speaker?' – and then perform in that role. This can free you up from many of the concerns that otherwise can plague you.

For instance, you don't have to worry about what the audience thinks of you if you are not being yourself. If they don't like the person they see, that's fine – because it isn't you that they're judging.

Sometimes, students worry that this means they are being inauthentic. But the truth is we all play roles all of the time. As long ago as 1956, the noted sociologist Erving Goffman even wrote a book about it, called the *Presentation of Self in Everyday Life* [6]. We don't speak to our parents in the same way as we speak to friends or to a university lecturer. This is ok. Navigating different environments and people is a skill set. It doesn't mean you aren't being true to yourself.

So, if it helps, let go of the pressure of speaking as you and instead be someone else when you present. Your audience will accept this, even if they know you, because subconsciously they already know that most people play a role when they are in front of an audience.

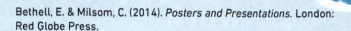

Further reading

Bethell, E. & Milsom, C. (2014). *Posters and Presentations.* London: Red Globe Press.

Goffman, E. (1990). *The Presentation of Self in Everyday Life.* London: Penguin.

Van Emden, J. & Becker, L. (2016). *Presentation Skills for Students* (3rd ed.). London: Red Globe Press.

References

1 Bruskin Associates. (1973). What Are Americans Afraid Of? *The Bruskin Report*, 53, 27.
2 Raja, F. (2017). Anxiety Level in Students of Public Speaking: Causes and Remedies. *Journal of Education and Educational Development*, 4(1), 94–110.
3 Griffin, J. & Tyrrell, I. (2003). *Human Givens: A New Approach to Emotional Health and Clear Thinking.* Chalvington: HG Press.
4 Gilovich, T., Savitsky, K. & Medvec, V. H. (2000). The Spotlight Effect in Social Judgment: An Egocentric Bias in Estimates of the Salience of One's Own Actions and Appearance. *Journal of Personality and Social Psychology*, 78(2), 211–222.
5 Singer, T. & Lamm, C. (2009). The Social Neuroscience of Empathy. *Annals – New York Academy of Sciences*, 1156, 81–96.
6 Goffman, E. (1990). *The Presentation of Self in Everyday Life.* London: Penguin.

10 Managing group work

I once asked a group of students why they thought we set them assessed group work. The answer came back immediately:

'Because you're evil'.

In my experience, this accurately sums up the attitude of a lot of students towards group work – or at least group work when it is being assessed.

Group work happens all the time, in classrooms in most universities. Every time a tutor or lecturer asks you to discuss something in a small group or sets a problem for you to work on with your peers, that is group work. It's also group work if you're a drama student and you're rehearsing a play with your classmates. Very often, these learning activities cause little to no problems for students at all, but somehow assessed group work seems to be able to cause all kinds of problems and stresses.

There are two significant contributing factors that tend to make assessed group work more difficult.

The first is that for a piece of work like this, you will be working in a group for a much longer period of time than you would, for example, in a classroom discussion. This means that you have to sustain the group for longer and there is more time and space for things to break down.

The second issue is the fact that the work is being assessed. The pressure to get a good grade and competing desires within the group can create conflict, frustration, stress and disappointment. In some cases, it can even harm friendships and negatively impact wellbeing.

In this chapter, we're going to examine the purpose of group work and how you can make it work for you and your peers.

What is group work for?

As we've already discussed in this book, grades can pull our attention away from the true purpose of our time in education – to learn. Research has shown that group work can significantly improve and deepen student learning [1] and also boost motivation and the likelihood that students will complete their programme [2]. Working with your peers to better understand content, analyse problems and develop solutions increases your learning by a significant and measurable margin.

One of the key lessons from this is that co-operative learning produces better results overall than competitive learning. We learn more by working together, and learning is often a social activity. This is one of the main reasons that your lecturers are tasking you with assessed group work projects. If the group runs well, you will know and understand more about your subject than you would have if you'd been taught and assessed in other ways.

The other main reason you will be asked to work in a group is that this is a skill that you will need once you have graduated. There are very few jobs where you don't have to work with other people at some point. Workplace teams are often beset with all the problems that you can encounter in group work. Sometimes, people don't pull their weight, some people try to control everything, and teams break into cliques and conflict gets in the way of productivity. Knowing how to work in groups, even when they are not functioning effectively, is something you will need in your life beyond your degree. It is much easier and safer to learn how to manage all of this while you are a student than when you are in the workplace.

That's all very well but it shouldn't impact on my grade!

This is a common refrain from students who don't like group work, because they've worked with group members who have let them down with a resultant negative impact on their grade. (Or they've managed to save their grade but only by doing their peer's work as well as their own and feel unfairly treated.)

This can seem deeply unjust. If you've put in more work than someone else, it seems unfair that their grade is benefiting from your work. Or if you've done everything expected of you and someone else has dropped the ball, it can seem unfair that this results in your getting a lower grade.

But the reality is that this is exactly what it can be like in the workplace – and there the consequences can be more severe than getting a lower grade. It is better to learn strategies for managing these issues now. When you are a student, every grade can seem like the most important thing in the world, but, as we discussed in **Chapter 4**, grades are not the most important thing. What you learn is far more important.

If you emerge from a piece of group work with a slightly lower grade but far more able to work in a team and with the skills and knowledge to address problems in teams, then you are much better off.

Remember, you don't go to university to accumulate grades – you go to learn. Learning like this will make you more employable and confident in the workplace.

Just as important, if you focus your group work on this learning, it will cause you much less stress and frustration. Rather than seeing problems in the group as barriers to a grade, you can view them as positive opportunities to try out strategies and develop your skills. Focussing on learning will improve the impact that group work has on your wellbeing and your own development.

Choosing your group

If you are given the opportunity to choose who will be in your group, it can be tempting to pick your friends. However, this isn't necessarily the best strategy. Your friends may well be like you and have similar strengths, preferences and skills. As a result, your group may be missing some key abilities and interests. For instance, you may have no one in the group who is good with technology or literature searches. This can cause you to struggle to cover some tasks at which none of you is naturally confident. It can also cause conflict because no one will want to be assigned those tasks.

Even more importantly, you may be denying yourself the opportunity to learn from a peer. One of the main benefits of group work is that you can work alongside someone who is strong in an area where you feel less confident and so learn from their expertise.

Instead of settling for your friends, take a moment to think about the task you have been set and what skills might be needed in the group. If you can, encourage your classmates to take a similar approach and to take some time to put together their groups, so that none of you feels rushed to do this. Taking time at this point can help all of you to avoid conflict later.

What if being asked to choose a group makes you anxious?

There can be many reasons why being asked to pick groupmates can make you anxious. You may not know anyone in your class or be able to identify people you feel comfortable with. You may find social situations difficult and find the prospect of approaching someone overwhelming. You may feel stressed by the prospect of rejection if you ask to join a group. Or it may just bring back bad memories of not being picked for teams at school.

All of these feelings and responses are very common. The reason most people choose friends and people they know for group work (with all the potential problems this brings) is that it allows them to avoid these awkward feelings. If you just pick your friends or the people next to you, then you don't have to risk rejection or get up the nerve to start a conversation with someone you don't really know.

It can help to accept and recognise that these feelings are completely normal and ok, but, as we've discussed in earlier chapters, you don't have to let them dictate your behaviour. Don't let the anxiety convince you that you are being forced to take a major risk. Yes, this may be uncomfortable – it may even feel a little painful – but it can't hurt you in the long term. Take a moment and breathe – it may help if you use a little 7/11 breathing (see Chapter 3) or another calming strategy that you find helpful.

If you are finding the situation particularly difficult, you may wish to ask your lecturer for help. But whatever happens, keep in mind that you will be in a group once the choosing process has finished. Anxiety may try to convince you that you will be left by yourself, but other students in your class will need people in their group. Even if it takes a while, you won't be left on your own.

It may help you to try to think about this as a strategic process rather than a social situation. As we discussed above, the best approach is to put together a group of people with complementary strengths and interests. Think about the task you've been set and the mix of skills you might need in your group. Then think about which of those skills and interests you possess – this doesn't mean you have to be an expert, just that you'd be happy to pick up those tasks. You can then use this to start conversations with your classmates.

For instance, you might say, 'I'd like to do task x in my group, is there anyone who doesn't want to do that or who wants to take on some of the other tasks?'

Don't get put off if you don't find a group immediately, and remember you aren't looking for a group of people to be your friends forever (although that may happen). This is just about finding a group you can work with this time – so you can learn more about working in groups. If the people you end up with aren't a perfect fit, this is an opportunity to learn how to make that situation work. The experience you gain, however successful on this occasion, will stand you in good stead in the future.

Setting up your group – getting things right from the start

Groups often go wrong because people within them don't share clear expectations and understanding about how the group is going to work. If one person expects everyone to spend 10 hours a week working on the project and to post updates every night and a teammate expects to work only 2 hours a week and post updates once in that time, then this may well lead to conflict.

Taking some time to agree the rules of the group, at the very beginning, can help to avoid this conflict and the stress and frustration that come with it. Students often know this but still don't have the conversation. This is perfectly understandable. In the workplace, formal meetings, with agreed terms of reference and a clear structure, are common. But these arrangements are supported by the structure and culture of the workplace. It is easier to be formal if your boss is in the room and you are in an official meeting room. In group work, you are sitting down with classmates and so agreeing rules and holding formal meetings can feel false and uncomfortable. Nevertheless, it is worth persisting even though it can feel odd.

With people that we know, we usually negotiate how we communicate and relate to each other implicitly. That is, we sort it out without ever really speaking about it directly. This is usually fine in social friendships but when there is a piece of work to be shared and completed, it is better to make the implicit explicit. Take time to discuss how you will work together, how you will communicate and what rules everyone will abide by. The worksheet below may help you and your group to address this. Using the worksheet can give the conversation some structure and using it as a task to complete together can help you to avoid some of the awkwardness that may arise in this discussion. If you aren't confident about taking control of this yourself, you might like to suggest to your groupmates that they read this part of the book as a way of making a start on the project.

Group work project plan – agreeing terms of reference

1   **What is the task?** Does everyone in the group have the same understanding? Take time to discuss this and let everyone speak.

2   **What about this task makes each of you excited, bored, nervous or happy?** Understanding how each of you views the task – what fires you up and what switches you off – may shape how you approach it and assign tasks.

3   **What do you each want to get out of this task?** Are you focussed on learning? The grade? Just getting it done? If there are differences between you, can you agree an approach that everyone is relatively happy with?

4   **How are you going to work together and separately?** What are the ground rules? Think about what might happen if someone can't meet a deadline you've all agreed or if someone is ill and so on.

5   **How often will you meet?** Does anyone in the group have other responsibilities that may influence this? This has to work for everyone.

6   **How will you meet?** Does it have to be in person or can you do this online? What are the rules for how meetings will be conducted? What are the rules about how you will feed back on each other's work to ensure it remains constructive?

7   **How will you communicate with each other outside meetings?** Does everyone have the same access to the method of communication? Is everyone in the group familiar with how to use it? What are the backup ways of communicating if the main method doesn't work?

8   **How often will you communicate?** Does anyone in the group have other responsibilities that may influence this? Again, this has to work for everyone.

9   **How are you going to start this task?** What are the first tasks that need to be addressed?

10 **How will you decide who is doing what?** How will you ensure that everyone feels this is fair? Democratic voting can sometimes work but it can also make someone feel ganged up on if they never get what they want.

11 **Who will co-ordinate?** You may want to elect a chair or take turns in chairing the group.

12 **What other roles do you need to make the group work?** If money is involved in the task, do you need a treasurer? Do you need a secretary?

13 **How will you plan the project through to the end?** Will you agree this at the beginning or develop it during the project? If the latter, this will need to be structured very carefully.

14 **What if something isn't working?** If you aren't happy about how some aspect of the group is working, how will this be addressed? Think about what might happen if someone isn't pulling their weight or if someone is being too controlling.

15 **How will you celebrate?** When the job is done, how will you mark the group's success and note what you've all learned?

The best laid plans of mice and men...

It is rare that any project goes exactly according to plan. As a result, it is important to regularly review your progress and alter your plans on the basis of the reality of where you are now. Once you have a project plan in place, it can be all too easy to stick to it come hell or high water. You'll have spent time building this plan, you've all committed to it and you may even have been able to visualise exactly how it would work. Giving up on it can seem like a compromise and a lowering of your standards. However, we know that successful groups are actually good at knowing when to cut their losses [3]. Flexibility is often the key to doing well. Take time in each of your meetings to review whether you are on track according to your original plan, whether you need to change what you are doing to stay on track or whether you need a new plan.

Check in with the group

You will also benefit from regularly reviewing how well the group is working together. Even if you've agreed ground rules and expectations at the beginning, people may have changed their minds or may feel differently now that they are seeing things work in practise. This isn't unreasonable, and a successful group will take account of people's feelings and readjust where possible. It can be worth asking – is everyone still happy with the ground rules? Do we all still feel that the deadlines are reasonable? Are our communications working well? Is anyone unhappy or uncomfortable with anything?

Raising concerns

If you have concerns about the way someone in your group is behaving, then it may well be right to raise this with them. Allowing niggles and dissatisfaction with each other to linger can result in bad feeling building up within the group and sometimes derailing things right before the project is due.

The most common concerns in group work are either that someone isn't pulling their weight or that someone is pushing people too hard and being too demanding. In either case, having a calm conversation about what is going wrong and how you can all work together to put it right gives you the best chance of getting the right outcome.

Be aware of your own emotions in this scenario. You may well feel frustrated or irritated with others in your group and this can make you want to blame them. Although this may give you some brief cathartic relief, it is unlikely to lead to everyone in the group wanting to work happily together afterwards.

Whenever people feel blamed, they tend to become defensive and to lash out or freeze in order to protect themselves. However justified you may feel in expressing your frustration, they are likely to feel under attack, triggering a fight-flight-freeze response. Remember the fight-flight-freeze response evolved to protect us when we were threatened by something that was dangerous to us. It is there to help us fight off threat and survive. So, when emotions are raised like this, you, and they, will be focussed on winning the argument no matter what harm is caused to your relationship. Neither of you is likely to be looking for solutions. This can cause your whole group to fall apart.

It is also worth bearing in mind that the assumptions we tend to make about other people's motives are often wrong. We find it easy to recognise when we haven't done something because we are very tired or because something urgent cropped up in our lives. When other people don't do something, we can assume it's because they don't care or are lazy – this is called a fundamental attribution error [4] and it is a common mistake we all make. Try to avoid making judgements about people's motivations until they've had a chance to explain them to you.

Instead, it can often be more productive to calmly identify what is happening and why this is causing a problem. Try to stay away from describing a groupmate's character and instead focus on their behaviour. For instance, if you feel they aren't pulling their weight, don't be tempted to call them lazy. Saying something like this is an attack on their whole character – you are criticising them as a person. This leaves no room for possible change or improvement. You are more likely to get a better response by saying something like 'I'm concerned that the work you promised hasn't been done yet and that if it isn't done soon, then that will impact on everyone else in the group'. This identifies the very real problem but doesn't say that they are a dreadful person. It also points the way to what they can do to put things right – complete the work as agreed.

If you can stay calm and avoid apportioning blame but still be clear about what the problem is, you are much more likely to guide your group to a solution that means you can all continue to work together productively.

When the group disagrees

Disagreements during group work are common and probably to be expected. It would be unusual if everyone in the group took the same views and shared the same vision, throughout the project, on everything. This is one of the reasons it is so important to set the group up properly at the beginning. If you have already agreed how you will raise and address disagreements, it makes them easier to tackle and easier for everyone to accept when they happen.

Disagreements in group work can feel entirely negative, but if you can focus on the true purpose of group work, they can become opportunities for learning. Rather than seeing any conflict as an irritant or barrier, see it as a chance to experiment and develop your skills.

When disagreements do happen, it is important that everyone stay calm and stay focussed on the problem, not on each other's character. There are a number of steps you can take to manage this situation. If you don't feel comfortable doing this yourself, you may want to share this guidance with someone in your group who does feel more confident to chair these discussions.

1 Try to be clear about everyone's point of view. Sometimes, disagreements can arise because of misunderstandings in communication rather than any real difference on substance. Ask people to clearly set out their view and repeat it back to them to make sure you and everyone else has understood it correctly.

2 Identify where you agree, so you are clear about what is shared between you all and what you don't disagree about.

3 Focus on the future. Try to keep the discussion away from what has happened before as this can lead to a situation in which people stack up disagreements, making it more difficult to find a positive way forward. Come back to the task you have been set and how you want to fulfil it.

4 Remember why you are here. Group work can become intense, and as a result people can lose perspective. This piece of work

has been designed to help you learn more about your subject and about how to work in a group. Try to stop it from becoming bigger than that and bring the focus back onto what is important.

5   Understand everyone's interests and see if you can work together to find a solution that satisfies all of them. Bring the conversation back to the original objective of the project as solid ground everyone can stand on. Compromise can be a good solution but can also result in a situation in which everyone is unhappy because no one got what they wanted. Ask questions – why does each individual want to do what they want to do? What do they think that will achieve that other people's ideas won't?

6   Let people be creative. The solution you need to resolve this may not be any of the ideas that people are offering now. Ask people to let go of their preferences for a short while and to brainstorm other ideas – set a rule that no idea is too daft and encourage people to speak off the top of their head. Even if what they say doesn't provide a solution, it may provide a spark of an idea that someone else can capitalise upon.

7   If things become heated, take a break. If people are emotionally aroused, they won't have the mental capacity to find solutions. If possible, take a 20- to 30-minute break during which everyone changes their environment. Go outside, breathe and calm down. Then return to the conversation.

8   Plan. Together try to build a new plan that keeps your whole group as happy as possible. Remember the reality – this is one piece of work; you will have to meet the deadline and then this will be over. Give people the opportunity to say whether there are still things they aren't happy with. If you can't find any other solutions right now, ask everyone in the group to give the problem some further thought before the next meeting. Recap what has been agreed and what the plan is now – it is important that, whatever has been agreed, everyone commit to it and to making it work.

Once the work is done – taking control of the experience by reflecting

As this chapter has reiterated, group work is useful because it deepens your learning and increases your skills. However, this learning can be lost if you don't take time, at the end of the project, to clarify what you have gained. We also know that reflecting on difficult situations and taking time to extract positive lessons from them can make you less prone to stress in similar situations in the future [5].

Sometimes, as part of the assessment, you will be asked to complete a reflective piece of work on your role in the project. If this is the case, take full advantage of this opportunity to clarify and embed what you have learned into your memory and build your confidence for future group work.

If you haven't been set this as a piece of assessed work, it will still be a useful exercise. The worksheet below can help to give this self-reflection some structure.

It may help to leave a day or so in between the completion of the project and completing this exercise. Whether your experience has been fantastic or difficult, your immediate emotions will make it more difficult to reflect objectively on what has happened. Give yourself time to switch off and to let your emotions settle; then block out some time to think about what you've gained.

As always when completing a piece of self-reflection, it may be difficult to find the answers at first. Take your time with each question and don't just settle for the first thought you have (e.g., 'I didn't do anything well'). Think over the whole project and try not to find answers that are just comparisons with others in your group. Focus on what you did, what you learned, what you gained and what you can do next time.

If in completing this exercise you recognise that there are skills you would still like to improve, seek out support from within your university to do this, whether these skills are to do with the project itself or with relationships and working in a team. Most universities provide extra support via study skills advisors or tutors, or you can search the internet for educational guidance to help you.

Group work – self-reflection

1   What went well for the group?

Did the group complete the project on time? When did you work well together? Did you plan well or overcome disagreements?

2   What role did you play?

How well did you work in the group? Did you help others to get along? Were you quiet – did you follow others or did you lead? How would you define your role?

3   What did you do well?

What did you bring to the group? What did you do that you were pleased with?

4   What didn't go well for the group?

Were there things you didn't get done? Did you have disagreements?

5   What could have made the project better?

How could the process and the product of the project have been improved?

6   What could you have done better?

Are there things you would do differently next time?

7   What did you learn about your subject?

This may not be just new facts – are there things you understand better now?

8   What did you learn about working in a group?

Was anything unexpected? Did you try out any new skills for the first time?

9   What role would you like to play in a group next time?

Would you like to be quieter or more reserved? Would you like to take the lead on something?

10 Are there skills you would still like to improve?

Would it help if you became more assertive or were better at listening to others? Would you like to get better at project planning?

Further reading

Goleman, D. (1996). *Emotional Intelligence*. London: Bloomsbury.

Hartley, P. & Dawson, M. (2010). *Success in Groupwork*. London: Red Globe Press.

References

1 Kuh, G. D., Kinzie, J., Buckley, J., Bridges, B. & Hayek, J. C. (2007). *Piecing Together the Student Success Puzzle: Research, Propositions, and Recommendations*. ASHE Higher Education Report, No. 32. San Francisco: Jossey-Bass.
2 Springer, L., Stanne, M. E. & Donovan, S. S. (1999). Effects of Small-Group Learning on Undergraduates in Science, Mathematics, Engineering, and Technology: A Meta-Analysis. *Review of Educational Research*, 96(1), 21–51.
3 Kahneman, D. (2012). *Thinking Fast and Slow*. London: Penguin.
4 Ross, L. (1977). The Intuitive Psychologist and His Shortcomings: Distortions in the Attribution Process. In L. Berkowitz (Ed.), *Advances in Experimental Social Psychology*. New York: Academic Press, 173–220.
5 Seery, M. D., Holman, E. A. & Cohen Silver, R. (2010). Whatever Does Not Kill Us: Cumulative Lifetime Adversity, Vulnerability, and Resilience. *Journal of Personality and Social Psychology*, 99(6), 1025–1041.

11 When things go wrong

Over the course of a three- or four-year degree, it is inevitable that not everything will work out exactly as you had hoped – and most of the time that's ok. In fact, in the long term, it can often turn out to be a good thing. Dealing with adversity can sometimes help us to develop skills and strengths that make us more able to respond to future challenges [1]. That doesn't mean you should expect to bounce back immediately from every setback. Turning something that has gone wrong into something that is helpful takes practice, time and insight, but it is a skill that you can learn and develop.

Let's take as an example something that happens to many students at some point in their academic careers.

Imagine that you have an assignment to complete for your course. You want to do well and so you work really hard. You spend a lot of time researching, developing and writing up your work. By the time you have finished, you are very hopeful that you will get an excellent grade. But when you get the assignment back, the grade is a lot lower than you expected – maybe you've even failed it.

Now, how do you respond?

I've conducted this little thought experiment with many students, and a number of responses crop up regularly – crying and drinking a lot of alcohol are up there among the more popular choices. Popular but not necessarily helpful.

Mistakes are a part of learning

The way we respond to setbacks very often depends on the expectations we place on ourselves. If you expect to never get anything wrong, to always get good grades, to never make a mistake and to be able to do everything required by your course before you've been taught it, then getting a low grade can seem like an utter disaster.

But the truth is that mistakes are a crucial part of learning and discovery. Trying something, getting it wrong, learning from your mistake and then trying again is how learning often takes place. The history of scientific discovery is based on people making assumptions, then testing them, realising they were wrong and building on this new knowledge.

Thomas Edison is a good example of this. In attempting to perfect the light bulb, he tried thousands of materials that didn't work before finding one that did. He also came up with numerous inventions that simply didn't work. When asked about his thousands of failures, he replied 'I have not failed 10,000 times— I've successfully found 10,000 ways that will not work'.

Or take the example of Alexander Fleming. He set up petri dishes in his lab to grow bacteria for scientific investigation. On returning from holiday, he discovered that some of the petri dishes had been contaminated by a mould that had killed off the bacteria. He had effectively ruined these specimens and damaged his research.

When I tell this story to students, some of them cover their heads at this point, and one had even stated that if that had happened to them, they would just want to go home and hide under their pillow. It's lucky for us that Fleming didn't do that. Instead, he sought to learn from his mistake and investigated the mould that had killed off the bacteria – in doing so, he discovered penicillin, the first antibiotic. In the years since, antibiotics have saved millions of lives – it's possible your life may even have been one of them. Luckily for all of us, Alexander Fleming wasn't a perfectionist.

Responding to things going wrong

None of this is to say that the desire to cry or sooth yourself with alcohol, chocolate or ice cream is wrong. You aren't weak for feeling upset or disappointed. Emotions are ok. It's what we do next that makes a difference.

When something goes wrong, we actually go through a process of responding – although we may not notice it. Our individual responses are often caused by habit or a desire to stop the unpleasant emotion that we are experiencing. We can drift into unhelpful behaviours so quickly that we may not even notice it happening.

If we can become more aware of our own responses (more mindful) and understand the possible options open to us, it is possible to change the way we respond to things going wrong. We can learn from our mistakes and so use adversity to make us stronger.

Take a look at the diagram below.

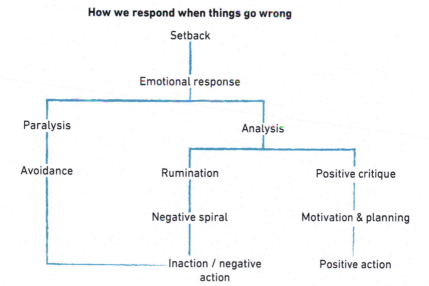

How we respond when things go wrong

As you can see, the first response to a setback is always an emotional response. There isn't anything we can do to change this (nor do we need to change it). Emotions happen more quickly than thoughts, and attempting to stop or control them usually makes them feel worse. As we discussed earlier, fighting with emotions can leave us feeling anxious about the fact that we are anxious or upset because we're upset. Instead, it is usually more helpful to accept the negative emotion and work with it.

If you got a lower grade than you'd hoped, it is ok to be upset, angry, disappointed, worried or frustrated. As we've already discussed in Chapter 3, the emotion is just doing its job. It's telling you that something important has just happened and is focussing your attention on it so that you can do something about it.

It may help to simply recognise and accept what you are experiencing. (You might even find it helps to say out loud to yourself or a friend 'I am upset and that's ok'.) Facing what you are feeling rather than trying to stop it will help you to take control. Taking control is important because, as we've already seen, negative emotions can drive us to do things that actually make us feel worse in the long term.

Avoidance

Take a look at the left-hand side of the diagram above, the part labelled 'Paralysis'.

One of the things that can happen when something goes wrong is that we try to pretend it didn't happen or shut down emotionally and hide from it. As we've already seen, this is actually a perfectly understandable response. Being upset, disappointed or anxious is an unpleasant feeling. As human beings, we are programmed to avoid pain wherever possible. Pretending that you haven't just received a disappointing grade, hiding it away in your bag in your bedroom and just not thinking about it can reduce those unpleasant sensations or even cut them off entirely – for a short period of time.

Avoiding things that are unpleasant is an instinctive response and something we all do to a greater or lesser extent. The problem is that avoiding things doesn't make them better and stores up more problems for the future.

Let's think about that assignment with the poor grade, for instance. Hiding it away and not thinking about it anymore means that you are depriving yourself of the opportunity to learn from your mistakes. Even more importantly, you're depriving yourself of the feedback your lecturer has provided, which will identify where you went wrong and how you can do better next time and all the times after that.

Those who study education identify that receiving and responding to feedback are among the most important elements of effective learning. Some even go so far as to state that without feedback, learning cannot take place. So if you don't read and think about the feedback you have received, you are cutting out a huge proportion of the useful learning that you need to be a successful student. Using feedback is also a skill that gets better with practice; the more you try to use it, the better you will get.

As we can see from the diagram, avoidance ultimately leads to inaction or to negative actions that can actually make the situation worse. You learn nothing from what has happened and as a result you are likely to repeat your mistakes next time and get a similar disappointing grade.

Of course, persuading yourself to read and engage with the feedback straight away may feel very difficult. (For instance, in **Chapter 3** we discussed how anxiety can emotionally hijack us and make thinking more difficult.) So, the first step for you may not be to start reading the feedback straight away. Instead, you may need to give yourself a little time and use some of the techniques described in **Chapter 3** to help you reduce the emotional arousal you are experiencing, so you can think clearly again. Once you have done that, you can begin to think about where you went wrong, learn from your mistakes and be ready to perform better next time.

Rumination

Take a look back at the diagram on page 159. This time, we are going to focus on the middle pathway, under the title 'Analysis', that leads to 'rumination'.

Sometimes, when something goes wrong, we don't avoid thinking about it and instead we find it preoccupying our thoughts – a lot. But thinking about it doesn't necessarily lead us to learn from our mistakes, particularly if the type of thinking we are engaged in is what we call rumination.

Rumination is essentially going over and over the same thing in your head, focussing on what has gone wrong and not taking positive action. Instead, you just keep thinking about how awful it is and how awful it feels and all the awful consequences that are now going to befall you because of what has happened. You may also find yourself identifying some possible steps forward but finding flaws in them or feeling unable to make a decision about which step to take first and so end up not doing anything that is helpful.

Sometimes rumination can work in a spiral. For instance, I once worked with a student who described an anxiety spiral that went like this. 'I spoke to my lecturer at the end of class. The way she spoke to me seemed strained and distant. I immediately thought 'she doesn't like me! She's going to mark my work extra hard. She won't help me if I'm struggling. I'm going to fail her module. That means I'll fail the year. I won't get a degree and I'll never get a good job!''

The truth of that particular circumstance? Her lecturer had a headache and was worried it was about to become a migraine. She seemed distant because she was in pain, not because she didn't like the student. But, in a matter of moments, the student's anxiety spiral had gone from recognising that her lecturer seemed strained to 'I'll never get a good job'. She then ruminated on that thought process for days until, with some encouragement, she spoke to her lecturer again and realised that her fears had misled her.

Other times, rumination may lead someone to pull together lots of small negative things to make one enormous, unsolvable, interlocking problem. Usually, these thoughts focus on either the world being unfair and impossible or the individual not being good enough. So a poor grade can lead someone to think 'It's because I'm a rubbish student. I'll never be good enough. It's why I don't have a girlfriend. No one likes me. I should just leave university before I make a complete fool of myself'.

The important thing about rumination is that it too leads to either inaction or negative actions to make the immediate feelings stop. While you are worrying about never being good enough, you aren't learning from your feedback or taking steps to improve your performance. Rumination doesn't help you solve problems; it just exacerbates them and makes you feel worse.

A useful question to ask yourself if you are unsure whether you are ruminating or trying to understand a problem is 'How is this thought helping me?' If you can't identify how it's helping you, you may well be ruminating.

Action

Now take a look at the right-hand side of the diagram, the side that flows through Positive critique and Motivation and planning.

Learning from our mistakes and developing new skills, insights and resources require some thinking and some work. However, once you are over your initial disappointment or upset, this process can actually be very rewarding and (depending on the circumstances) even enjoyable.

Moving beyond self-blame or avoidance, ask yourself what you can learn from what has happened. You may find it helpful to use the action planner in the box below to help you find a positive and structured way forward.

Take your time with this and don't expect to be able to go from the emotional reaction to positive action in moments. You may need to give yourself some time for the initial emotional impact to subside. Sometimes, it can help to allot a time period to recover before trying to move on. For instance, you might say to yourself, 'Ok, I can be upset for the rest of today but tomorrow morning, I'm going to sit down and look at the feedback properly'. Or 'Ok, I can be annoyed until 3 pm, then I'm going to sit down

Action Planner – When Things Go Wrong

1. What has gone wrong?

_____

_____

How bad is it really? How significant will it be?				
Not significant				Very significant
3 weeks from now	1	2	3	4	5
3 months from now	1	2	3	4	5
A year from now	1	2	3	4	5

2. Why did it happen? Can you learn anything from this experience?

_____

_____

_____

3. What resources/people can help you?

_____

_____

4. How can you make the situation better?

_____

_____

_____

5. When can you apply what you have learned?

_____

_____

with one of my friends or a family member, talk it through and build an action plan'.

This means you won't be trying to block the feelings, but you won't let them take control either.

Let's go back to our scenario of the assignment that got a poor grade and see how the action planner can help.

1   What has gone wrong?

Be clear about what the problem actually is – yes, you didn't get the grade you wanted, but why is that a problem?

Will the grade actually affect anything? How much impact can this one grade, when averaged out, really have on your overall degree? Grades for each piece of work usually account for only a tiny fraction of your final grade.

Your emotions may have convinced you that this is a disaster, but the practical effect may be negligible. Scaling and scoping the problem can help you decide how big a deal it is really.

2   Why did it happen? Can you learn anything from this experience?

Read the feedback from your tutor and re-read your assignment to see if you can understand why you got a grade lower than the one you expected. Has your tutor pointed out areas in which you could improve? Do you understand these suggestions? And, if so, what could you do about them? Remember to think broadly about how learning and academic performance actually happen. You may perform better next time if you can improve your physical, psychological or social wellbeing.

Bear in mind that this isn't about finding reasons to blame yourself for what went wrong this time – mistakes happen in learning. It's ok that this happened as long as you use it as an opportunity to build your skills and understanding.

3   What resources/people can help you?

You may want to talk to your tutor to get further clarification on your feedback. Or you might find it helpful to talk to a study skills advisor or a librarian. It may also be useful to speak to your peers; learning from each other is a valuable part of the university experience.

4 How can you make the situation better?

This might be about things you can do to make yourself start to feel better today or about building your skills and learning to ensure that you get good grades in the future. It may also be about dealing with any uncertainty the poor grade has caused. If you have failed the assignment, find out what that actually means and what you now have to do. Uncertainty is usually much more difficult to deal with than the consequences.

Pick one or two steps to start with. Remember, this may be about taking action to address how you feel – like spending some time with friends or giving yourself permission to do something that boosts your wellbeing. Your aims are to reduce any emotions that may hijack you and to build up your motivation to take positive action.

Once you feel ready, you can focus on learning from what has happened. If possible, choose something that will be easier to start and that will give you a sense of momentum. That may mean choosing something that you find easy or interesting or that you may enjoy.

As you build on each step, take time to recognise the new learning that you have acquired and how you have improved your knowledge and understanding of what is required to succeed at university. By taking positive action and recognising your new learning, you will build your confidence and your skills. As a result, the poor grade can lead to a positive outcome.

5 When can you apply what you have learned?

If there is another assignment coming up soon, try to apply this new learning to how you approach this piece of work. If that isn't the case, it may help to set yourself some tasks based on what you are learning at the moment. Could you write a short essay on something you've recently studied in class? Is there a subject that interests you that you could research more as a way of improving your search skills?

The sooner you are able to apply your new learning, the more likely it is to become embedded in memory and habit and the better you will feel.

Taking control of the process

Being able to respond to adversity, learn from it and move on positively takes practice, and no one manages to do it all of the time. If this isn't something you do now or you're someone who finds it difficult, just remember, the more you practise, the better you will get.

To begin with, you will probably find yourself repeating old patterns. You may find that you automatically move into avoidance or rumination. That's ok. If you realise that has happened, resist the temptation to be frustrated with yourself. The fact that you've recognised what has happened is a sign that you are already starting to make changes.

Simply accept that this was your response this time but that you don't have to let that dictate what happens next. Then do what you can to take control and move to the Positive critique side of the diagram. Actively engaging your thoughts and actions and doing what you can to learn and improve will make you feel better and perform better in the future.

Further reading

Duckworth, A. (2017). *Grit – Why Passion and Resilience Are the Secrets to Success*. London: Vermillion.

Syed, M. (2011). *Bounce – The Myth of Talent and the Power of Practice*. London: Fourth Estate.

Reference

1   Seery, M. D., Holman, E. A. & Cohen Silver, R. (2010). Whatever Does Not Kill Us: Cumulative Lifetime Adversity, Vulnerability, and Resilience. *Journal of Personality and Social Psychology*, 99(6), 1025–1041.

12 Facing the future

In 1974, a man called Philippe Petit walked across a tightrope from one of the World Trade Center's twin towers to the other. If you search for this online, you can find pictures of him, a balancing pole in hand, walking carefully across the wire, 1350 feet above the ground with no safety net.

When I'm facilitating workshops with final-year students, I use this image to talk about their future after university. This is because, very often, when students talk to me about what they think their lives will be like, it makes me think of M. Petit, on his tightrope, with the ground a long way below him. Many students seem to believe that their lives and careers will be just like his crossing: there will be one extremely narrow path to success, and any mistake, however small, will result in their complete doom.

It's a terrifying prospect and if that's how you think about your future, it's bound to make you nervous, perhaps even anxious. Fortunately, that isn't actually how your life is going to be. Our lives are not defined by how well we tread one narrow path, and mistakes will not result in your doom. Success does not happen in a straight line, and there are many different ways we can be successful.

Your future does not require you to traverse a tightrope to be successful.

So why do so many students in my classes agree that the image of M. Petit on the tightrope is a good metaphorical representation of how they feel about the future? It's because, at the moment, a number of dominant myths in our culture promote ideas that can make the future seem terrifying.

The power of cultural narratives

As we have already discussed, what we believe can have a very powerful effect on how we feel and behave. This is even truer when those beliefs are ingrained in our environment. When a narrative is repeated back to us over and over again, it is hard not to absorb it and come to believe it. This is because we are 'normative to our environment', meaning that we adjust our behaviours and thoughts to fit in with the culture around us. This is part of our evolutionary programming; it helps us to fit in with other people and our surroundings.

Much of this adaptation to culture happens without our even being aware of it. What time you eat your evening meal, how close you stand to other people and whether or not you hug acquaintances will all be heavily influenced by your culture. We can even find that our emotions are influenced by how other people around us are feeling.

When we become aware of this, we can make choices to break through these beliefs and behave differently. But this requires you to develop a high level of awareness about what you believe and what has influenced that. Sometimes, there are things that we believe are facts – but they aren't; we just think they are facts because everyone we know also believes they are facts. By confusing a belief for a fact, we can make decisions that aren't helpful to us.

For instance, Jared Diamond writes about a Viking colony in Greenland that appears to have died out, partly because of a lack of available food despite the rivers being full of edible fish [1]. The most likely explanation for this is that these Vikings came to believe that eating the fish was wrong – perhaps because they thought it would anger a god or because they believed the fish were poisonous. In this case, a belief (that people thought was a fact) resulted in a situation in which a community disappeared rather than eat the available food that may have kept the colony viable.

If everyone seems to believe something and they are all telling you the same thing, it isn't surprising that you come to believe it too. This is what has happened with many of the narratives about the world of work (and the future more generally). These beliefs are repeated over and over again, in the media, online, and by people around you, often without any evidence to support them and in some cases in the face of evidence that shows them to be plain wrong. Becoming aware of these narratives and choosing to act in the way that benefits you, rather than running with the herd, can be helpful for your future career and your wellbeing. In doing so, you can become the intelligent Viking, who ignored what everyone was saying, ate the fish and survived.

The myths about your future

So let's take a look at some of the most common myths that many final-year students have to negotiate. We'll discuss them a little bit here and then take a closer look at how you can overcome them later in this chapter.

Great careers are planned in detail every step of the way — so now you should plan out your whole life.

Having a sense of where you are going and what you would like to do in life can be very helpful. Many students experience real anxiety as they finish their degree, precisely because they have no idea what they want to do next. So, giving over some time to thinking about what you want from your career and how you want to impact upon the world is a sensible thing to do (below we'll look at some ways of doing this).

However, this does not mean you have to accurately plan every step of your life from now on. When you think about what you want to do next, you aren't planning the rest of your life. If you allow yourself to think that you are, you can quickly become overwhelmed because this is an impossible task. You can also become worried that if you make the wrong decisions now, you will ruin your whole life. This can result in your becoming paralysed with indecision.

The truth is that the future is impossible to predict. We have no way of knowing how things will work out, and that isn't how people's careers tend to develop. Most of the successful professionals that I know (including me) aren't in careers or roles they ever planned to be in. Life develops in unexpected and exciting ways that can't be guessed at in advance.

All you are doing now is deciding what direction you want to take and what the first steps in that direction might be. If it turns out that the first step doesn't work out, it is perfectly possible to learn from this, change direction and move on successfully. It doesn't have to be a disaster – as we can see from our second myth.

You must get the perfect job as soon as you graduate.

It is doubtful that there is any such thing as the perfect job. Even those of us lucky to be in careers we love will still have days when we feel frustrated, bored or overwhelmed. Hunting for perfection is also a trap: it can lead to your not considering jobs that would be good or feeling disappointed because you can't find something that perfectly fits your expectations. It is better to have a sense of where you would like your career to go and then to look for a job that would be a reasonable step in that direction.

Even if the first job you get bears no relation to your ambitions and is just to pay the rent, there is still no reason to despair. Most graduates don't fall into fantastic jobs at the first time of asking. That doesn't mean they don't go on to have great careers.

The career you choose is the one you'll have for the rest of your life – so choose well.

The general estimate now is that most people will change career several times between beginning work and retirement. You aren't stuck with your first choice, and as a graduate you will have skills, knowledge and wisdom that will make switching careers easier. Your ability to learn will mean you will find it easier to retrain or learn about a new sector. If you choose a career and find you hate it, you can learn from that, rethink, make a new plan and work towards a career that fits you better. Picking one route forward now does not mean you will be trapped forever. So breathe. If you don't have absolute clarity about what you want to spend your life doing, that's ok. It's something you can work at over time and even if it takes a few years, you can still find a career and life that work for you.

Careers are competitive – you can't afford to let up for a moment or you'll fall behind.

There are very, very few instances where this is true. In any case, many people don't discover what they really want to do until a few years after university. You can afford to make some mistakes – as with being a student, as long as you keep learning from your mistakes, you will be able to build a fulfilling life and career.

Being successful and buying the right things will make you happy.

There are now many studies that demonstrate that once you have enough money to comfortably get by, there is a decreasing boost to your wellbeing from each increase in your wealth [2]. In other words, if you are in poverty, extra money can really boost your wellbeing. But beyond that, piling up money, possessions and titles can't buy you happiness. Instead, happiness comes from leading a fulfilled and balanced life in which all of your needs are met.

Unfortunately, most of us in the Western world live in a consumer culture, in which we're encouraged to believe that happiness is something we can purchase. Just look at the number of adverts that encourage you to buy something – from chocolate to mobile phones – not because the product is good but because (they say) it will make you feel better. This is so ever-present that resisting it can be difficult – even though we know it's not really true, we still find ourselves believing it.

Being conscious of this when planning your life and career can help you avoid jobs that will make you miserable but that you might otherwise take because they pay a little bit more. Of course, you do need to earn a reasonable salary, but focussing on a role that will be meaningful and fulfilling will lead to a better life overall.

Happiness is all very well, but in the real world you have to sacrifice happiness just to survive – there is no other option.

This myth, or some version of it, is usually offered as plain common sense. It suggests that the desire to have good wellbeing is somehow naïve and foolish – that if you honestly believe it is possible to have a career that you love and to be happy in your life, then you will soon learn the truth. It is a miserable way of looking at the world. It also leads to dissatisfaction with life and unhappiness generally.

It is possible to have a career that helps you to meet your needs, provides you with a sense of purpose and makes you feel you are contributing something of value to the world. You might not get all of this in your first job, but if you keep your focus on things that have real value to you and you continue to strive, you will have the opportunity to get there.

You are entirely defined by your job/career.

Undoubtedly, our careers are important. You will need to earn money to survive and if that is the case, you may as well spend the time doing something that adds to your wellbeing overall. However, your career is not your life; it is only part of your life. To be able to meet all of your underlying needs, you will need to maintain a balanced lifestyle outside of work.

This balance will probably be different for different people. But if, for you, spending much of your time with family and friends is the most important thing, then it is perfectly ok to choose a career that facilitates that. You are not obliged to move away from your family or have no time to see them just to pursue a career that is less valuable to you than the people you love. When you think about your future, it is important to think about the life you want to lead, not just the job you want to do.

The robots are coming and they're going to take all of our jobs.

Versions of this idea have been around now for decades. The truth is that technological change does result in changes in the types of jobs we do – there aren't many roles for typists or blacksmiths these days. But that doesn't mean there won't be possible careers for you in the future. There will always be doom-laden predictions about the future, but change also brings with it opportunities.

The important thing is to be flexible in thinking about the types of roles that you could do that would still be fulfilling for you – which brings us back to thinking about meaning, pleasure and strengths.

Back to meaning, pleasure and strengths

Back in Chapter 6, we looked at Tal Ben-Shahar's model of meaning, pleasure and strengths [3]. If you haven't read that section yet, it's worth going back to look at it now.

At any point, now or in the future, when you think about your career, it is worth returning to the exercise we set out in Chapter 6 and doing it again, listing those things that give you meaning and pleasure and that use your strengths. Our interests, pleasures and abilities change over time, so you may find new things appearing on your lists and some things disappearing.

Having an ongoing sense of those things that give you meaning, pleasure and a sense of competence can help you to keep shaping your career towards roles that are fulfilling and support your wellbeing.

However, there is obviously one final category to consider when doing this for your career – what can you get paid for? Although, as we explored above, money can't buy happiness, you will need to be able to pay for a roof over your head and food in your fridge – and for a fridge. Generally, though, I would recommend that you consider this category last. First, identify the things that give you meaning, pleasure and use your strengths and then think about what jobs or careers will match your list and pay you a decent salary. This will create a new Venn diagram for you.

Applying this last practical consideration can help to keep your ambitions rooted in the reality of where you are right now. This isn't to say that you shouldn't be ambitious – if you want to change the world, then do – but even if you want to change the

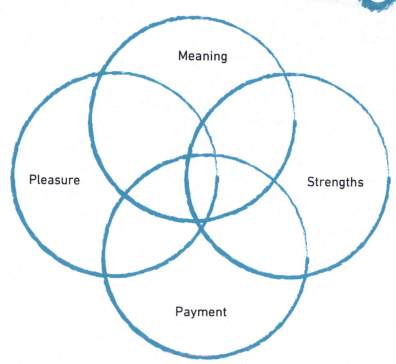

world, you have to start by acknowledging the reality of how things are now. Then you can identify the first steps that you need to take, confident that the decisions you are making are realistic but leading to an ambitious end.

It's highly likely that your first job won't land right in the middle of your Venn diagram. But at least by considering the four elements on the diagram, you can aim for roles that are as close to the centre as possible, depending on what opportunities you have. Then, over the course of your career, you can work from where you begin to where you want to be.

Putting off happiness until later

One of the ideas that you may encounter is that, in your early career, you should be willing to sacrifice your wellbeing and happiness to work long hours, have little social time and generally live a life out of balance so that later you can be happier. In other words, by doing this, you will progress in your career and then get to a point when you will have the money, standing and role that will allow you to be happy. This is a risk – many people take this gamble and find that it never pays off. Instead, they just spend years being unhappy and when they get to the moment they were expecting it to bring results, they find that the rewards weren't as fulfilling as they expected.

This is not to say that you should never make sacrifices in your career. Sometimes, working long hours, on a meaningful task, does bring long-term rewards, and hard work, in itself, can bring benefits. But be mindful about what you are doing. Ask yourself – is this definitely going to be worth it? Is this taking me in the direction I want to go? Will this journey be focussed intrinsically or extrinsically?

Setting goals – what model to choose?

Another way of thinking about your future is to think about the goals you want to set yourself. There are a number of goal-setting models that you may well come across and you may find helpful (e.g., SMART goals: specific, measurable, achievable, relevant and time-based), but it is wise to be careful about these and the idea that achieving goals, in itself, will lead to life satisfaction or happiness. There are a number of reasons for this:

1 By focussing on clear 'achievable' goals (what you or other people think is achievable), you can unintentionally reduce your ambitions. Judging what is achievable or realistic is very difficult when you are trying to predict a career or your whole life. Very often, we are capable of much more than we could initially believe, but we achieve it in small, incremental steps. Each step may seem perfectly achievable in the moment, but predicting the whole journey, at the beginning, may seem wildly optimistic. Don't let goal-setting rob you of the ambition you really want to follow.

2 Many goal-setting models will ask you to identify tangible goals that can be measured. It is much easier to do this for extrinsic goals (such as job titles or roles, salary, and size of office) than for intrinsic goals (such as a sense of fulfilment,

caring about your teammates, and a passion for your work). But, as discussed in Chapter 5, we know that focussing mainly on extrinsic things reduces our wellbeing whereas having a mainly intrinsic focus is good for our wellbeing. Don't let a model push you away from valuing your intrinsic motivations.

3 Goal models can encourage you to set arbitrary timetables by which you should have achieved certain things. This can set a trap for you. You might achieve amazing things but believe you have failed because you haven't stuck to your original timetable. You might turn down great opportunities because they weren't on your original plan and a deadline you've set for yourself is looming. This practice also ignores the fact that many things aren't in our control – your plan to be in 'job X' within 10 years may not be achievable if there are only a few of those posts and the people in them don't want to move on. Success may appear in ways you haven't predicted and on timescales you couldn't guess.

In essence, using the wrong goal-setting models for you can be risky because they can funnel you down one narrow pathway, limiting your ambitions and reducing your flexibility. That isn't to say that planning for your future is impossible or pointless. Drifting through life and hoping that something might turn up can also lead to poor wellbeing and dissatisfaction. Instead, it can help to focus on the kind of life you want to have and the impact you want to make on the world. Then you can build a flexible plan to work towards this that allows you to respond to unexpected opportunities and doesn't result in your judging your success or worth against an arbitrary set of standards or deadlines.

One of the ways you can do this is to separate out 'do' goals from 'be' goals.

'Do' goals and 'be' goals

Former US Secretary of State Henry Kissinger once said that there are two types of ambition: the ambition to do something and the ambition to be something [4]. The ambition to do something might be an ambition to reduce inequality, cure cancer or create an amazing piece of music. The ambition to be something might be an ambition to be prime minister, a famous research scientist or a pop star.

When we talk about ambition or building successful careers, we often talk about 'be' goals. 'Be' goals are easier to measure and feel like a more solid thing to aim for. It is easier to say 'I want to be a teacher' than to say 'I want to help children learn, grow, achieve and be happy'. The first sounds like a solid and respectable ambition. The second sounds like a vague set of woolly aspirations to do good, that may be slightly naïve and unworldly.

But this conception of those two goals is entirely driven by our current cultural perspective. There is nothing vague or unworldly about wanting to help children learn, grow, achieve and be happy. In many ways, it is one of the most important things you could do and it is something that as a society we need. It is also a task that requires a high level of skill, knowledge, strength and commitment and therefore is deserving of respect. It is also something that you can do in more than one way – becoming a teacher is simply the most obvious.

This is not to say that having a 'be' goal is always wrong or that having a 'do' goal is always right. If the thing that you want to 'be' will meet your underlying needs and intrinsic motivations, then that is great. If the thing you want to 'do' is gain power so you can invade other countries and make people fear you, then that is probably bad for you and, more importantly, for the people you want to invade.

But thinking about your goals in this way can help you to be sure that you are focussing on building a life and career that are suited to you and that will be good for your long-term wellbeing. It can help you to avoid ending up in a career that other people may think is sensible but that will make you miserable.

It can also give you different ways of thinking about your future if you are not sure what career or job you want.

You can do this following this simple exercise. Think about the goals that you have in your head – separate them out into 'be' goals or 'do' goals. Start with any 'be' goals you might have and ask – why do I want this goal? You can use the worksheet overleaf to help you.

'Be' goal	Why you want this goal	Is this goal intrinsic or extrinsic?	'Do' goal	Why you want this goal	Is this goal intrinsic or extrinsic?

Take your time and try to be honest with yourself. You will probably have a number of different reasons for each goal. Or it may be that once you think about it properly, you aren't sure why you've landed on that goal at all – maybe it was something that someone else suggested to you or it's what other people you know are doing. Again, this is an exercise that is beneficial if you spend some time on it. Try to move beyond the first thoughts that come up.

When you've identified a few reasons why you want that goal, take each of those reasons in turn and ask yourself whether they are motivated extrinsically or intrinsically (or a mix of the two). Again, remember that extrinsic motivation isn't always wrong, but it is better if the balance in your life is tilted towards intrinsic motivations.

If you want to 'be' something entirely because you believe it will bring you the respect of other people or because it will allow you to buy expensive things, then you will probably find that you are aiming for a career that ultimately will leave you dissatisfied. Research has shown that, although it is important to have a sense of achievement in life, being able to tick off extrinsic goals doesn't tend to lead to greater happiness. The extra things and the views of others can feel quite hollow if they are all you have.

Now do the same exercise for your 'do' goals.

When you have done this, bring together all of those things that you placed on either list and that were intrinsically motivated – those things that were driven by your passions and interests, that gave you pleasure or that made you feel you were doing something valuable or useful. Then think about what careers might help you to meet these goals. If you already had in mind a career that definitely matches these intrinsic motivations, then that's great. But don't stop with just that one idea.

The real benefit of separating out 'do' goals from 'be' goals is that it allows us to approach the future in a more flexible and open way. If you identify that you want to 'be' something, whether it be prime minister, a pop star, a research scientist or a structural engineer, then there is only one way to meet that goal. If you do not succeed in getting that role, you risk setting yourself up for failure – and being so aware of the risk of failure that it prevents you from achieving what you are capable of.

However, if you pay attention to your 'do' goals, there will probably be more than one way of achieving them. This doesn't mean you have to abandon the idea of becoming prime minister, a pop star, a research scientist or a structural engineer; it just means that you have that as one of a number of potential options that will allow you to meet those goals. It also means that when you manage to land that role, you will already know what you want to do with it. You will still have further goals to keep you intrinsically motivated.

In the main, it can help if you have a few large, intrinsically motivated 'do' goals that you can work towards over your whole career. These may be goals that you can never totally achieve but that you enjoy and are pleasurable to work towards.

Let me explain how this works for me. I believe that our university students are far more stressed and distressed than is necessary or helpful. I believe a university should be a place where students thrive, grow, achieve and have good wellbeing. Everything I do is geared towards achieving that goal – be it in therapy, teaching, my research or writing this book. Will I achieve that goal by myself? Absolutely not. But by working with brilliant people in the higher-education sector, I can make a contribution, and I get meaning and pleasure from doing so. Keeping a focus on this big goal allows me to be flexible and open to new opportunities that come along. Working towards your future in this way is something we call Planned Happenstance.

Planned Happenstance

Planned Happenstance theory [5] sets out why the straight-line narratives about how careers are constructed are wrong and offers another, more realistic way of thinking about our careers.

As we've already highlighted, the future is unpredictable and most people have careers that take unexpected turnings and opportunities. The path to success is rarely predictable or simply planned. Things will happen that you didn't expect – you won't get some jobs you want, some jobs that you do get won't be as enjoyable as you'd hoped and you will be presented with amazing opportunities that you never could have predicted.

Planned Happenstance theory suggests that rather than developing one rigid plan for your career, you accept from the beginning that the future is unpredictable and work with that knowledge. In this way, you will be ready to adapt to changes in the workplace and your life and to make the most of what comes along. This doesn't mean simply waiting around for the right opportunity to come up. Making the most of Planned Happenstance requires active engagement with your career – not only do you need to put yourself in the way of possible opportunities, you also have to develop the skills, knowledge and experience required to take advantage of them when they do arrive.

To prepare for the future, you need a sense of the kinds of opportunities you will want to seize when they present themselves. You also need an awareness of how to identify these opportunities and you need to ensure you have developed the skills, knowledge and understanding required to be the one who gets those opportunities.

This is why it is so important to think about what you want to do in the world, what motivates you intrinsically, what you find meaningful and pleasurable, what you are good at and what makes you happy. Understanding all of this will provide you with a solid platform from which you can build your future. Then you can start to work towards careers that match you as a person and will support your wellbeing. If you continue to learn and grow throughout your career, more opportunities will present themselves. But remember, they might not be the opportunities you expect.

To make the most of Planned Happenstance, there are a few things that can help.

- Throughout this book, we looked at the importance of focussing on learning. This continues to be true when you move into the workplace. Stay curious, seek out opportunities to develop and use the ability to learn that you developed at university.

- Don't dismiss opportunities at first glance. It may not be the most obvious route to the role you initially had in mind, but would you find it interesting, purposeful or enjoyable and might you learn from it in ways that are helpful? Does it still meet the meaning, pleasure and strengths test?

- Meet other people who share your large goals and passions. Finding like-minded individuals or communities can help you improve your learning and build social connections. It can also ensure that you are involved in work that leads to the kinds of opportunities that will benefit you.

- Accept that some choices won't work out as well as you'd hoped. This isn't a disaster, it's just a stage on the journey and a chance to learn. If a role isn't right for you, it's ok to leave it but take some learning with you. What wasn't as good as you'd hoped? Is there some aspect of this that you thought you'd love but didn't? How does that change your perception of what you want to do? In light of all of that, what would be better? Now use this learning to make some plans and find a better role for you.

Life beyond your career

As we discussed above, a career is important but it is only one aspect of your life. Spending some time thinking about the life you want to live is also important. This can be challenging and even scary. If you've always been in education, the prospect of stepping out of that structure can seem unnerving. For the first time, there isn't a ready-made lifestyle, environment and routine to step into. You will no longer be in classrooms every day, and the route forward is much less clear and obvious. Feeling a little bit of worry about this is perfectly normal and something that many students experience. Change can feel unsettling, and leaving university and stepping into the world outside are very significant changes.

However, change can also be exciting and freeing. You are now in a position to have much more say over how your life goes. You are no longer confined by the academic timetable and the next assessment. You can choose your structure, lifestyle and environment. You have freedom to add to your education and ability. But to be able to do this well, you need to think about who you are now and the life you want to live.

This can feel like a big thing to contemplate. But again, it is important to remember that any decisions you make now do not lock you into anything forever. You can try things out to see how you like them.

Aristotle and the good life

We began this book by talking about early versions of wellbeing, including Aristotle's [6]. As we've already discussed, in his work, he talks of eudaimonia, often translated as happiness or flourishing. He suggests that this is achieved by living a 'good life' in balance. In some respects, this is what we all want. To be happy or to be flourishing is the ultimate aim for all of us. All the things we want to have, be or do we want because we believe they will make us happy or lead to our flourishing.

Whether those things we want are extrinsically motivated (like a shiny new sports car) or intrinsically motivated (like love), we want them because we think they will make life better. We want them because we think they will make us feel better. As we have discussed in these pages, some of these things will work really well and some much less well.

This is why it is important to consciously think about these things in advance. The tools and models that were put into this book to help you maintain good wellbeing as a student can equally apply to your life after university. So, using whatever model of wellbeing works for you, it can help if you try to visualise what kind of life would allow you to flourish and be happy.

When we start thinking about a life that would make us happy, it is easy to imagine a scenario in which you win the lottery, never have to work and get to spend all of your time having fun. But we know that a life like this isn't much good for your wellbeing in the long term. As Aristotle knew back in the fourth century BCE, pleasure and happiness are not the same thing. Of course, pleasure and fun are important, but we also need purpose, a sense of autonomy and security, and a genuine connection with other people.

Finding balance can be challenging, but you are more likely to find it if you plan for it and make decisions, consciously thinking about how you can achieve it. Again, this doesn't mean you should expect to be able to create this life straight away; it may take time and work to get there. But keeping it in your mind can help and can prevent you from drifting into lifestyles that are bad for your wellbeing overall.

Tips on visualising your future

Using visualisation techniques can help you to more clearly see what you want from your life and career. One of the key elements in this is not getting too hooked up in trying to predict the details accurately, being 'realistic' or rushing to dismiss thoughts as unlikely. Instead, you need to give your imagination permission to do its job. This is usually best accomplished if you can first get yourself into a relaxed state. You may find that the following exercise helps to do this:

1   Sit or lie somewhere comfortable, where you won't be disturbed for a little while.

2   Close your eyes and begin by focussing on some aspect of your body. You might notice your back against the bed, chair or floor or how your arms feel, or you might notice your feet.

3   Then pay attention to your breathing. At first, don't try to change this. Simply notice if you're breathing high into your chest or low and slow into your stomach.

4   Now gradually let your out-breath become longer than your in-breath. Don't force it, just gradually and gently elongate your out-breath. If it helps you can count and aim to breathe in for 7 seconds and out for 11.

5   As you begin to relax, imagine yourself in a place in nature. It can be a place you've made up or a real place. Pay attention to what you can see, hear, smell, touch and taste and allow each thing you notice to help you relax.

6   When you feel ready, let your imagination carry you forward into a future in which you are leading a fulfilled and balanced life. This can be as unrealistic as you want. Pay attention to what you are doing – in this imagined future – where do you live? Who else is there? What kind of job are you doing? Why do you enjoy it? What do you do in your spare time? How do you maintain your wellbeing?

7   Allow these elements to fix in your memory. Then, when you are ready, gently move your limbs and slowly open your eyes to bring yourself back into the present.

8   Now take a moment to note down the details of the life you just imagined.

9   Having done that, take a step back from your imagination. The life you conjured up may never be completely possible – but that doesn't mean you can't learn from it. What was it about that life that so appealed to you? Why did the elements of that life make you feel fulfilled, flourishing and happy? Are there other ways of getting those same elements into your life plans?

10 It may help to do this a few times and imagine a number of different futures and then to note the common elements that come up.

Preparing for the transition out of university

Taking the time to think about all of this can also help you to prepare for leaving university. When you come towards the end of your degree, it isn't unusual to experience a range of competing emotions. This is perfectly understandable given the levels of uncertainty that can accompany the end of your time at university. You may not know what you will be doing immediately afterwards or where you will be living. Your social group may be moving to many different geographical destinations. You may not be certain about your finances, and while all of this is in your mind, you will still be in the process of completing your final course work or preparing for exams or both.

The important point to remember is that this is normal. Every year, millions of students all over the world face the same circumstances. As time moves on, they find their feet and everything slots into place. The same thing will happen for you. This period of uncertainty is temporary – it will pass. But it will do so more quickly and easily if you spend time specifically thinking about and planning for the transition itself (as well as thinking about your future career).

It can be all too easy to get to the point when you've handed in your final piece of work and completed your exams and then suddenly find yourself managing lots of changes happening around you. This can make the transition more difficult and anxiety-inducing and can also make the end of university feeling like a huge and disappointing anti-climax.

Naturally, the way that the end of university affects you will depend on your own personal circumstances. There are different adjustments to be considered if you are a mature student with a family or a 21-year-old student with no dependents. This can also shape the way you think about the end of university as it approaches. If you have lots of other responsibilities, not having to find time to study any more may seem like a relief. But if you have nothing concrete to occupy your time in the weeks after term ends, the next few months may seem empty and without clear purpose.

Whatever your circumstances, the transition out of university remains a significant event that will benefit from some thought and planning. Here are some general things it may be useful to think about as you approach the end of your studies. Feel free to ignore anything that isn't relevant to you or your circumstances – but think about whether there are other things that you would substitute instead.

1 Celebrate

It is important to take the time to mark your achievements. Finishing a degree is a big deal. You've done it. Years of study and hard work have led you to this point and you deserve to take a moment to celebrate what you've done. Don't move past this moment as if it doesn't mean anything. It does. Even if you aren't 100% happy with your final pieces of work, you've still completed a university degree. Feel proud of that.

If you have friends at university, it may be good to get together with them to share this celebration. This doesn't have to mean doing something that costs a lot of money or having a huge party. Do something that is meaningful for your group. Celebrate each other's success together and mark the fact that you made it to the end.

2 Break the future into chunks

When you think about life after university, it can be very easy to think about 'The Future' as a vast formless entity that stretches out forever and that you somehow have to control and plan. This can leave you overwhelmed and paralysed with indecision. Of course, you need to think about your career and the kind of life you want to have – but you also need to think about what you will be doing next week.

Having some short-term plans, to get you through this transition, can help you to feel a greater sense of control and to avoid drifting. Making plans for what you need to do now can also help you to avoid feeling like your life has entered some kind of holding pattern over which you have no say. Think about what you need to do in the next day, the next week, the next month and the next 3 months. Some of this time may well need to be spent on planning your career and looking for a job. But you'll probably also benefit from planning practical steps (e.g., planning your finances) and maintaining a balanced lifestyle.

3 **Don't let the short term twist your view of the long term**
If you don't walk out of your degree and straight into a graduate job, negative thoughts can hijack the situation in unhelpful ways. You may find yourself thinking – 'I'm back where I was before I started my degree. What was the point? I've wasted time, energy and money'. This is a normal thought process in the circumstances but it isn't true.

Remember that you studied for a degree, not because it would land you the perfect job in weeks (or even months) but because it would open up possibilities for a different kind of life. That doesn't happen right away. The weeks after the end of university are unusual and temporary. Use the tips in this chapter to keep you focussed on the future you want and to take practical steps to get there.

4 **Stay connected**
Whether your main friendship group was composed of people you met at university or your friends are mainly people from outside university, the end of your course will still bring a significant change to the social structure of your life. Your timetable will have given you a structure and guaranteed regular contact with others – many of whom probably shared interests similar to yours. During the transition from your student life to whatever you do next, social connection with others is still important.

This can be particularly challenging if your closest friends are going to be spread apart over a great geographical distance. Social media can help you to stay in touch and not feel like these relationships have completely disappeared. But you will also benefit from face-to-face social contact. This might mean developing some friendships that haven't been as central until now – and that may mean spending more time with people from outside your university experience. Don't leave this to chance. It may help you to make a list of people whom you could still meet up with and plan out opportunities to spend time together.

Even if your friendship group remains relatively intact, it may still be worth thinking about whether the end of university is going to reduce the amount of time you are guaranteed to see other people. If so, think about whether you want to plan some things into your weeks to replace this time.

5 **Maintain a structure and balance (as much as possible)**
As we've already acknowledged, the end of university changes the structure of your social life. But it will also change the structure of your day-to-day experiences in other ways. Your timetable will have given you a solid framework around which to build the rest of your week. Academic work and deadlines will have given you focus, purpose and something to do. As we discussed in Chapter 5, we need a healthy structure in our lives to maintain our wellbeing. It can help if you recognise this and make plans to compensate for the loss of structure that your course gave you.

If the end of university is bringing a lot of changes, then it may be difficult to establish a new routine right away. Instead, it may be more effective to plan out each day and week in advance, making sure that each day has as much of a balance as possible between purposeful activity, fun and rest.

6 **Health care**
If you are moving away from the area where your university is based, remember to transfer your health care. You will need to move to a new GP in the area to which you're moving. If you have regular treatment for a long-term condition, speak to your health-care professionals about moving your support well in advance of moving.

7 **And, yes, once again, don't forget the basics**
Transition and change can easily throw out our healthy habits. Be aware of this and try to maintain a good diet, exercise and sleep. They will help you to maintain energy, motivation and mood as you move to the next phase of your life. Maintaining good habits during the transition out of university will also make it easier to transfer these good habits to the next phase of your life.

Rebel – a life in radical balance

As we discussed at the beginning of this chapter, pushing back against the narratives that surround us can be difficult. When these messages are repeated by politicians, the media, your family and your friends, it can be hard to resist them. They can seem like immutable rules that we all have to follow whether we like them or not. That is why resisting them is an act of rebellion. However, this is not a rebellion without reason or point. Instead, it is a rebellion that has both evidence and common sense on its side. It is also a rebellion that is good for you and the people around you.

Going along with the dominant narratives in our culture can be so much easier. It takes a lot less energy to just accept what everyone is saying and to do what you are 'supposed to do' – to work long hours, to ignore your health, to sleep badly, to spend most of your time on things that bring no meaning or pleasure, to accept dissatisfaction as inevitable and to spend less time than you'd like with your loved ones.

It takes much more effort to take control of your life, to stay focussed on what genuinely matters and to prioritise your wellbeing and the wellbeing of those you care about. But taking control in this way is much more likely to lead to a life of fulfilment, joy, achievement and happiness. By being willing to choose your own path, you also change the culture for those around you. You become part of the narratives they imbibe and, as a result, you can help to free them up to make good choices about their own lives.

This can be difficult and hard to sustain all of the time. Sometimes, we all succumb to the culture and the expectations around us – sometimes, it is necessary to do so. But when those moments have passed, we can resume healthy habits and push back again.

I've talked about Aristotle throughout this book because he was one of the first people (as far as we are aware) to write down that a good life was one lived in balance. He said, for instance, that courage was the balancing point between foolhardiness on one side and cowardice on the other. He also recognised that a good life comes from taking control of what we can and accepting what we can't. To an extent, we are all subject to the fluctuations of fate. You will have some bad luck in your life, you cannot predict the future and you cannot control where you came from or the opportunities you've had up to now. But you can work from whatever situation you find yourself in to make your life better. As a graduate, you will have more knowledge, resources and skills than most – even if it doesn't always feel like it. You can trust in yourself, in your skills and in the knowledge of what a good life entails.

There is much in your future that is uncertain but that does not mean that you cannot be confident about your ability to create a good life for yourself. Have the courage to live a life in radical balance, be kind to yourself, focus on things that have meaning and that bring pleasure and seek genuine connections with the people around you.

If throughout your life you try to meet your needs in balance, you are helping to make the world a better place. You will also be building a better life for yourself on solid ground, not walking on a tightrope in the air, worried that you might fall.

Further reading

Gardner, J. & Barefoot, B. (2019). *Step by Step to College and Career Success* (8th ed.). London: Macmillan.

Rook, S. (2018). *The Graduate Career Guidebook* (2nd ed.). London: Red Globe Press.

References

1   Diamond, J. (2006). *Collapse. How Societies Choose to Fail or Survive.* London: Penguin.
2   Kahneman, D. & Deaton, A. (2010). High Income Improves Evaluation of Life but Not Emotional Well-Being. *Proceedings of the National Academy of Sciences*, 107(38) 16489–16493. doi:https://doi.org/10.1073/pnas.1011492107.

3   Ben-Shahar, T. (2008). *Happier.* London: McGraw Hill – The Observer.
4   Dallek, R. (2007). *Nixon and Kissinger: Partners in Power.* New York: Harper Collins.
5   Mitchell, K. E., Levin, A. S. & Krumboltz, J. D. (1999). Planned Happenstance: Constructing Unexpected Career Opportunities. *Journal of Counseling and Development,* 77(2), 115–124.
6   Aristotle. (2011). Aristotle's *Nicomachean Ethics.* R. C. Bartlett & S. D. Collins. (trans.). Chicago: Chicago University Press.

13

Conclusion

Deep breaths and baby steps

One of the things you learn quickly when you work with students is that they are generally smarter and more capable than you. They certainly know more about being a student and have all the capabilities necessary to learn well and be well. It's just that sometimes circumstances get in their way.

The title of this chapter came from a student I worked with several years ago. We were reviewing the remarkable progress she'd made from what had been a series of difficult problems. I asked her how she thought this improvement had come about. 'Oh, it's simple', she replied, 'deep breaths and baby steps'.

This is something I've tried to remember ever since – for myself as well as for the students I've worked with.

We've covered a lot of different aspects of student life in this book. As we come to the end, I want to offer one warning and some final thoughts and tips.

The warning is simple. I've packed as many thoughts, suggestions and activities into this book as I can to help you have a good student experience. But please, don't try to implement them all and certainly don't try to implement them all at once. If you try to do everything I've suggested, you'll become overwhelmed. It will also be better for you if you can take the general lessons of this book and then apply them in your own way rather than simply trying to follow what I've written. Whatever you do to improve your learning and your wellbeing, it has to fit with who you are.

Remember, nothing works for everyone. If you try something from this book (or something you come up with yourself) and it doesn't work, it may make sense to try it a few more times. Sometimes, when things don't work, it's because of the particular circumstances of that moment. But if you try it a few more times and it still doesn't bring you any benefits, then maybe it isn't for you. That just means it's time to move on and try something else. If you keep experimenting, you will find things that work.

Small changes will add up to big changes. Keep focussed on what matters and aim for a better balance over time.

A few final thoughts

In summarising the main messages of this book, I want to focus on some key principles rather than the specific exercises and tips. Whatever you choose to do to improve your learning and wellbeing, they will be more likely to be helpful if you keep the following ideas in mind:

Positive change is possible (but sometimes may take a little time).

Most of the time, it is possible for us to do something that will improve our wellbeing and our learning. In the normal course of day-to-day events, there are simple things we can all do to meet our needs in balance, boost our health and learn well. This doesn't mean we can completely resolve all of our problems, make ourselves feel fantastic, no matter what is happening, or ignore reality. But taking as much control as possible and taking any positive practical steps we can take will make things better than they otherwise would be – even if only by a little bit. Remember, positive practical steps can be about things you do, but it can also be about the way that you think.

If you are in a really difficult situation, it may take a while for big change to happen. Sometimes, it can take a while for our emotions to catch up with our newer healthier behaviours or for us to find the thing that works for us, and, sometimes, we have to plan our way out of our circumstances over time. But it is important to believe that positive change can happen and will come your way – with a little work. Be hopeful; many students see great improvements that they didn't expect.

After all, being a student is about transforming your life for the better.

Students can enjoy university, be mentally well and learn well.

Being a student does not have to be bad for your mental health and wellbeing, and learning can be exciting, fulfilling and fun. This doesn't mean that every day will be great, that there won't be disappointments or that you will love every aspect of university life. University courses last a long time, and there will be ups and downs throughout that time. But don't let people talk you into believing that being a student is inevitably stressful. It will be challenging and stretching, there may even be some times of stress, but be open to the possibilities for fun, meaningful experiences, friendships and joy that being a student can bring.

Negative emotions are ok.

Sadness, anxiety, anger and other negative emotions are not harmful in themselves and cannot hurt you. When they are an appropriate reaction to something that has happened to you, they are doing something for you. They are bringing your attention to something important, helping to keep you safe and encouraging you to look after yourself. Accept your negative emotions, listen to the messages they are giving you, thank them and then decide how correct they are about the situation you are in and what would be most helpful for you to do now.

No one knows how to do everything straight away. Students can learn and get better at being students (and at life).

If you haven't been a university student before, there is no way you could know how to be one right away. Don't be misled by your extrovert peers who seem to know what to do. Everyone has to learn the art of being a student – you have to learn how to learn at university level and how to make student life work for you. Your journey through this will be unique to you, but the more proactive you can be, the easier you will find it. Give yourself permission and time to learn how to be a student and to be well and learn well at university. Taking away the pressure to be able to do everything straight away will mean you will learn more quickly.

The basics matter – breathe, sleep, eat healthily, exercise and enjoy time with friends.

Neglecting your physical health can be easy to do when you are busy but it will have a significant impact on your wellbeing and your ability to learn and perform academically. We've discussed this several times because it can affect so many aspects of our lives. Set good habits to maintain good physical wellbeing and, when in times of difficulty, try to be even more aware of looking after yourself physically. Good sleep, a healthy diet, exercise and balance will help you to have the resources to manage and overcome any problems you encounter.

We go to university to learn, not to acquire grades.

If you can focus on learning, as much as possible, you will make your academic experience more personally meaningful and fulfilling and therefore good for your wellbeing. Wherever possible, try to engage in deep learning, linking your subject to the things you find important and drawing on your intrinsic motivations. It is what you learn that will be of most benefit to you in the years after your degree.

But remember, you do still need to be aware of reality. If you have an assignment deadline, make sure you meet it. If that means stepping away from deep learning for a while, this is fine. If you have other obligations that reduce the time you have to study and sometimes have to take more of a surface approach to survive, then that is perfectly sensible; you will still benefit from

whatever you manage to learn. There is no way to do this perfectly. But the more you can focus on learning, the better.

Using support is a great skill to have and one you can improve.

Your university wants you to be successful. That's why they have resources in place to help you to be successful. Depending on where you are studying, the nature of this support will vary, but it will help you only if you use it. Whether that support comes from your lecturers, your tutors, librarians, study skills teams, careers advisors, counsellors, student services/affairs professionals, chaplains, staff in halls of residence, online support or your peers – making use of it will help you improve your academic skills and look after your wellbeing.

If you feel uncomfortable asking for help, that is ok. Being independent can often be very helpful – but as with everything else, there is a balance to be struck. Learning to ask for help isn't a sign of weakness, and you aren't being a burden. We all need help sometimes. You can learn to get better at asking for help. Start small. Consider what would you find easier: asking someone you know for help? Or asking someone in an official role in your university? You might want to practise with a small request for help first and then, when it feels more comfortable, to ask for more support. Working with a counsellor while you try to develop these skills might also be helpful.

The future is not a tightrope – you do not have to be perfect to create a life that makes you happy.

Do not let yourself be persuaded by the narratives in our culture. Life does not proceed in a straight line, so don't set yourself the task of making your life go in one undeviating direction. Embrace the unexpected opportunities that come along, be open to change, learn deeply and be aware of what is important to you. Of course, practical things matter, you will need to earn a living and keep a roof over your head. But there will be ways you can

do this that you find to be fulfilling and meaningful. Plan to live a life that meets your needs in balance.

One step at a time.

Improvement often comes from small changes, taken one step at a time. It can be easier to sustain small changes that build into big changes. You don't have to transform your life overnight or achieve some kind of perfection. Any improvement is an improvement, no matter how small. Once you've embedded a positive change into your life, you can build on it and add another. Step by step by step, you can create a day-to-day life in which you can be well and learn well.

Remember the words of my student; deep breaths and baby steps can take you a long way. So identify your first step (or two), take a deep breath, believe in your ability to do this and step forward.

Remember, you have a whole university supporting you. You can do this.

Good luck and as the old Irish proverb says, 'May the road rise up to meet you and may the wind be always at your back'.

Ideas I want to remember

What's the idea?	What page number is it on?	Notes

Index